the wider place

the wider place

...where God offers freedom from
anything that limits our growth

by EUGENIA PRICE

TURNER
PUBLISHING COMPANY

Turner Publishing Company
Nashville, Tennessee
www.turnerpublishing.com

Cover design: Bruce Gore

Library of Congress Cataloging-in-Publication Data Upon Request

9781684426522 paperback
9781684426539 hardback
9781684426546 ebook

17 18 19 20 10 9 8 7 6 5 4 3 2 1

In gratitude for every still strengthening memory of one of God's great men, my beloved friend and editor, Peter de Visser.

acknowledgments

Scripture quotations are from the King James Version and the Amplified Bible (Zondervan).

Grateful acknowledgment is made to the following publishers for permission to quote from these books:

To Harper and Row for the quotation from the address by Harold H. Anderson entitled: *Creativity as Personality Development* included in the book *Creativity and Its Cultivation* (addresses presented at The Interdisciplinary Symposia on Creativity, Michigan State University), edited by Harold H. Anderson. Copyright © 1959, Harper & Row.

To Farrar, Straus and Giroux for permission to quote from *The Ability To Love* by Allan Fromme. Copyright © 1965, Farrar, Straus and Giroux.

To Elizabeth Yates McGreal and E. P. Dutton and Co. Inc., for permission to quote from *Up The Golden Stair* by Elizabeth Yates. Copyright © 1966, E. P. Dutton and Co. Inc.

To Zondervan Publishing House for permission to quote from *Your Teen-ager and You* by Anna B. Mow.

contents

PART I

Chapter 1.   God Is Still Alive and Free   17

Chapter 2.   Where Is The Wider Place?   25

Chapter 3.   What Is Freedom?   37

Chapter 4.   Who Needs More Freedom?   47

PART II

Chapter 5.   Freedom From Confusion About God   57

Chapter 6.   Freedom for Whom?   67

Chapter 7.   How Do We Make Use of Freedom?   75

Chapter 8.   Do We Love Freedom or Captivity   85

Chapter 9.   To See Again   97

Chapter 10.   Out From Under   109

Chapter 11.   More Than a Sermon   121

PART III

Chapter 12.   Freed From Conformity and Rigidity   133

Chapter 13.   Freed From Mere Opinion   143

Chapter 14.   Freed to Be Natural   151

Chapter 15.   Freed From Indecision   159

Chapter 16.   Freed to Welcome Responsibility   167

Chapter 17.   Freed From Fear   179

Chapter 18.   Freed From Chronic Loneliness   193

Chapter 19.   Freed From a Meaningless Life   205

Chapter 20.   Freed to Receive Forgiveness   217

Chapter 21.   Freed to Ask Nothing for Ourselves   229

Chapter 22.   Free Favors Abound—in The Wider Place   241

about the writing of the wider place . . .

Our world fights and struggles for *freedom*. There would be no need for the struggle if man could bring himself to accept and begin to use the freedom God offers to everyone. If this seems a glib generalization, perhaps the reading of this book will show otherwise.

The acceptance and use of God's freedom must begin with Christians, and it is not uncommon at this point for the world to begin to laugh. We as disciples of Jesus Christ do not act as though we have been given inner freedom. We are too often bound by prejudice and bigotry and fear and doubt and dullness and condemnation and pietistic posturing. We need not be, and to examine the way out of this bondage is the intention of *The Wider Place.*

Perhaps, before the examination of the potential of this inner release, a word needs to be said about how we miss life in *the wider place;* how we choose—consciously or unconsciously, the partial bondage in which we find ourselves.

Sooner or later most of us reach the point in our lives where we must choose either to follow blindly the patterns of our conditioning, conforming to our special groups' emphases so as not to be an outsider, *or* to enter—alone with God, if necessary, *the wider place* where we dare to permit God to set the standards.

If we choose, at this crucial point in our lives, to follow the herd merely for protection and acceptance, we begin the respectable, sure road to bondage. When God sets our goals and supplies the criteria for our judgments and our interests, we are in the *free* place where he intends us to live. And the free place is *a wider place,* where there are no limits on our souls, our minds or our spirits but the creative limits of God himself.

Too many of us fear that if we *think,* we are not exhibiting faith. This is a little ridiculous. God created our minds, and the human mind open to God, choosing God's way of freedom and love, cannot escape—faith the kind of tough, elastic, durable faith that produces courage and balance and maturity.

Those who dare to enter it will find there is *action* in the *wider place* with God. The gifts of the Spirit do not produce a state of stagnant passivity. God's Spirit liberates and his freedom is *truth in action* in our behalf, and through us, in behalf of those still groping about in the confinement of darkness.

This is a book with deep meaning for me. One which I hope will create a healthy discontent among those who have too long been satisfied with a fixed, pinched concept of God, unaware of the true nature of the totally creative, totally redemptive freedom he offers.

It is a book for all people who need to choose the way of love with more vigor, more determination, and to choose it more often.

The Wider Place is a book about liberty—not license. And it is the product of a distinct change in the pattern of my own life after having followed Jesus Christ, however haltingly, for almost seventeen years. It is an attempt to share some of the results of the new freedom which has come from a firm decision to slow down, to find time and privacy in which to learn to listen to God himself—to learn of him and of myself in relation to him. To learn something of myself, not as a public figure, but as just another human being pursuing her craft in a daily way, with neighbors she knows by name, with grocery lists, a garden, a few close friends of her own choosing—and time to think.

As with the completion of each new manuscript, I once more, first of all, thank my mother, who not only sustains me by her faith, but who has taught me so much about real freedom, by leaving me free to be myself. My deep thanks also, to my beloved friend, Joyce Blackburn, who gives as much unselfish attention to my manuscripts as she gives to her own, and with whom I feel I am able to think as clearly, or more clearly, than when I think alone.

Dr. Anna B. Mow has again given me the valued, loving service of checking my content and of supplying many valid suggestions—all of which I took. I am indebted to Marjorie Hoagland for research in the Library of Congress, and to Frances Pitts and others who shared their freeing experiences with me and who have prayed for me as I wrote.

Mr. Floyd Thatcher of Zondervan Publishing House has given me not only unselfishly of his time and editorial energies, but of his encouragement and friendship. It is to his real help-meet, Harriett Thatcher, that I owe the discovery of the pertinent Daniel Webster quotation on liberty, which formed one of the strong themes of the book.

My dear friend and neighbor, Elsie Goodwillie, can never be adequately thanked for her skillful management of the typescript and for her personal caring that we both make it our best effort.

One final word now that it is finished: the writing has convinced me that *the wider place* of freedom in God is so wide, we will all forever be convinced that we are always just entering.

Eugenia Price

St. Simons Island, Georgia
April, 1966

PART I

God grants liberty only to those who love it.

Daniel Webster

So if the Son liberates you—makes you free men
—then you are really *and* unquestionably free.

John 8:36 (The Amplified Bible)

GOD IS STILL ALIVE AND FREE

This is not a book to prove that God is alive or that freedom is necessary. It is a book to urge Christians to recognize not only their need for more of the freedom the living God longs to give, but to urge a more daring willingness to receive his gift of creative liberty. To urge us to walk strong in our confidence in God's forgiving love, out into the wider, freer place he has prepared for us.

1 / GOD IS STILL ALIVE AND FREE

THIS IS NOT A BOOK to prove that God is alive, nor is it a book to prove the necessity for the kind of spiritual freedom God offers.

Most of us are aware of the "freedom" claims made by the exponents of the "new radical theology." The more I read of the "freedom" of which they write, the more I become convinced of the liberty offered by the Son of the *eternally alive* God. There is nothing new about the periodic theological outbursts which seem to gain impetus by tearing down the old, rather than clarifying the *true*. Nietzsche was saying the same things almost a century ago. Where God is concerned, it is impossible to tear down the old or to discover anything radically new—except as life in God is always renewing itself. God is neither new nor old. He is the beginning and the end. The minds of *uncertain* people can be confused by theological tirades (old or "new") but God cannot be confused, killed off, or diminished. And no amount of declared "new freedom" found in any so-called "new" theology can really compete with the freedom Jesus promised when he said: "If the Son therefore shall make you free, ye shall be free indeed."

For man to claim new knowledge of God in no way changes God. He is just the same as he was yesterday and he will be the same forever. Men can propagate "new" ideas about him, can pronounce him dead, but in no way can he be changed. The minds of those whose faith in him is wobbly or secondhand can be changed, shaken up—even the faithful heart can be deeply disturbed, "wounded" as my mother expresses it. But God is eternal or Jesus was wrong, because he said, "I and the Father are One . . ." and ". . . lo, I am with you all the days,—perpetually, uniformly and on every occasion—to the [very] close and consummation of the age."

To attempt to find freedom by following an obscurely expressed, recondite philosophy which declares God dead and Jesus merely the example to be followed, seems a flat contradiction. How can Jesus be followed as trustworthy if he was wrong in the central purpose of his own earthly life? Every ounce of his energy and intellect was spent in revealing the nature of God, his Father, in revealing and demonstrating God's undying love, his intentions toward the human race he had created. Would Jesus have done this if God were going to die when the Son was crucified? Would he have said, ". . . I go to the Father . . ." if the Father were to be gone?

It is a mistake not to attempt to understand the very real discontent which motivates much of the thinking behind the "new" radical theology, and an equal mistake not to see that the living God is using it by forcing us all to rediscover what we do believe about him. If we have accepted the Trinity— the Father, Son and Holy Spirit—matter of factly, making little or no use of their energies in our lives, this radical declaration that God (the Father) is no more, can shock us into faith. We need the Father to be for us. We need the Son to be with us. We need the Holy Spirit to guide and counsel us—to be in us.

It is simply unrealistic that Jesus would have come to reveal a God who would no longer be there for us to turn to.

The "new" radical theology will not be wasted by the redeemer God, who wastes nothing. God is never in favor of closing men's minds. He welcomes controversy about himself. He is safe from it. No amount of intentional or unintentional shock statements can touch God except as they touch his loved ones. At the same time books are being written to declare God passé, other new books are being written from the viewpoint of *God's continuing revelation of himself in Jesus Christ.* So, God will win. He always does. He already has. Not as a victor over the vanquished, but as God, who loves everyone who argues on both sides.

Most of the young men who expound the "new theology" are in search of what they call freedom. Some seem merely in rebellion. Some of them are in transit. Some, I believe, will ultimately find freedom in the One who declared: ". . . if the Son shall make you free, ye shall be free indeed." Others among them will go on searching, attempting to make their own freedom. Surely, God is in favor of intellectual liberty, but just as surely, God grants *inner freedom* to anyone who wants it enough to assume the responsibilities that come with it.

God grants freedom because he is God. Only he knows the inestimable worth of freedom to his creatures. If God had not known the necessity of freedom, he would have created us bound to him without the ability to choose for ourselves. God's purpose in creation seems irrevocably tied to the absolute necessity for freedom in man. God longs for everyone to respond to his Creator in love, but knowing that any love response, if it is real, must come from a free choice, he created us free to choose. Free to decide for ourselves whether or not we will love God; will take the *freedom* he offers in the human life lived in his will and not ours.

Man searches for freedom in a thousand ways: God offers it for love's sake. Only God can offer freedom to the inner man, because only God knows man as he is. Only God can offer freedom, because only God is totally free.

Man, from the beginning, has contrived to bind himself. Our first parents thought they were grabbing liberation: they grabbed bondage. And until God sent his Son, Jesus Christ, "to announce release to the captives," no one was free.

God could send the potential of freedom to man through Jesus Christ because Jesus was as free as God. I have no fight with the "new theology" exponents as far as their right to believe as they choose, but I do decry any ideas of God which appear to lean toward the obtuse, the confusing. God's principal interest seems to me to be to make himself clear. He became a Man in Jesus Christ for this purpose alone. Only God knew that if man could catch even a glimpse of what He is really like, man's heart would be drawn to respond to Him in love. Not coerced—He leaves the human heart free—*drawn*. God became a Man for reasons we cannot begin to comprehend, but I am convinced he did it surely for the sake of simplicity and clarity. The theologians who speak only in the archaic language of Zion and the "new theology" exponents who seem to have to struggle to make their points clear to the average mind are both apt to create unfortunate confusion in us. To know and follow Christ is not always easy, but it *is* simple, because God came to earth to simplify—not to complicate.

God *could* send his Son to clarify himself to man because his Son was free to remain his wholly divine self, even in the midst of the hatred and cruelty and viciousness of man's world. If, as one young radical theologian wrote, "Jesus was an extraordinary man who chose to allow love to be the sole motivating force in his life," God's purpose collapses. I can't see that God could have afforded a chance on one merely mortal man (no matter how spiritually inclined and obedient) to demonstrate the Father's own intentions toward us. I can't see that God could have dared depend on even the most uniquely spiritual man on earth to "save his people from their sins." Men can *tell* other men about their need of a Savior, but no man can *be* a Savior.

The Savior, Jesus Christ, who came from the Father to *be* God's Word to us, could be counted on by the Father because Jesus Christ was as free as God to retain his own identity, even as he identified with man.

He was *free to turn from temptation*, because having been with God where there was all glory and no sin, he *knew* he would only be binding himself by yielding to any temptation on this earth.

Jesus Christ was *free to forgive* because he shared the very heart of God himself. The love of Jesus of Nazareth did not merely *resemble* the love of the Father, it was the same love.

He was *so free of prejudice* and the *need for personal prestige* and *acceptance* that he could call the motley collection of disciples he chose. He thought and acted in the freedom of his own identity and purpose.

Because Jesus Christ *was* God and Man walking our earth, he was free *to associate with discredited people* and know that his holiness could not be stained. He could treat women, even bad ones, as persons. He could treat social outcasts with dignity.

He was *free of the Law* because he was not only present with the Father when the Law was created, he saw its fulfillment in himself and could live above and beyond it.

In every crowd that gathered around Jesus when he taught and healed, were vicious critics of his teaching. Still he was *free* to heal and to teach.

"I am the way, the truth and the life," Jesus claimed. He was not pointing a way, or telling a truth, or instructing toward a better way of life. He claimed to *be* the way, he claimed to *be* the truth, he claimed to *be* life itself. He was free to make these claims because "without him was not anything made that was made," including the way, the truth and all of life.

And so, it is not then amazing that Jesus claimed that if *he* made a man free, that man would be free indeed. Through every day of his life on earth, Jesus Christ *lived* freedom. Particularly as he stood before Pilate, Jesus was free. Pilate was bound heart and soul with frustration and anger, but Jesus stood alone and serene in the midst of the violence and hatred of the mob, seeming almost to pity Pilate for being afraid to act according to his own conscience. Jesus was calm and in control because he was the *free* only begotten Son of God. They would kill his human body, but he was *free* to live again.

This is not a book to prove that God is alive or that freedom is necessary. It is a book to urge Christians to recognize not only their need for more of the freedom the living God longs to give, but to urge a more daring willingness to receive his gift of creative liberty. To urge us to walk strong in our confidence in God's forgiving love, out into the wider, freer place he has prepared for us.

WHERE IS THE WIDER PLACE?

The wider place is not swampy, with no boundaries and no definition. In no way does it contradict what Jesus said about the narrowness of the way that leads to life. Rather, awareness of the wider place seems to throw new light on what he really meant when he said: ". . . strait is the gate, and narrow is the way which leadeth into life, and few there be that find it." He didn't say the Christian life was narrow; he said, "narrow is the way which *leadeth into life*. . . ."

2 / WHERE IS THE WIDER PLACE?

I N MY OWN TIMES of meditation, of thinking, of prayer, the phrase "a wider place" comes again and again: the wider place directly related to inner freedom, to creative liberty—to the natural, personal release from bondage to fear, to general neuroticism—offered by Jesus Christ to anyone who truly wants it.

It is not as though I have "arrived" at any advanced state, or have discovered any "new ground" for faith. I don't seem involved in the wider place, except as I am permitted to wander deeper into it, all amazed, filled with more and more wonder that it is here available for earthlings . . . any earthling who counts steadily on God's commitment to us all. It is as though I have newly become *aware* of the almost dizzying *freedom* to be found there with God. The *freedom* not to fight back, not to indulge in self-pity; the freedom to dare not to be afraid because God is there. It is as though I have been given a *new*, sharp awareness of the bondage of prejudice, of indecision, of doubt, of the exclusive heart. And I find that I am just as keenly *aware* when, through an intentional or unintentional act or attitude, I suddenly drop out of the wider place. I am overcome with a kind of homesickness, an urgency to hurry back to the wider, freer place where God is *all*.

The wider place is not swampy, with no boundaries and no definition. In no way does it contradict what Jesus said about the narrowness of the way that leads to life. Rather, awareness of the wider place seems to throw new light on what he really meant when he said: " . . . strait is the gate, and narrow is the way which leadeth into life, and few there be that find it." He didn't say the Christian life was narrow; he said, "narrow is the way which *leadeth into life*. . . ."

Jesus said that he came that we "might have life and have it more abundantly." His words about the life in him are all affirmation. If we have turned to him, we already have life. The turning *is* a narrow way with a strait gate, there is no doubt of that. Any act that humbles the human ego, brings it to repentance, changes it from independence to dependence, is a squeeze—a narrow way. But I have never been aware of a narrow way *since* I received life from him. I have been many times aware of a squeeze from other people, but never from God. Now, after almost seventeen years as his follower, I am daily more aware of the wider place into which he is leading me. Faith in Jesus Christ should not breed masochism or the restricted life. It should breed liberty and joy. His first greeting to the disciples when he walked out of the tomb has been said to be translated more accurately as "Oh, joy!" rather than "All hail."

The wider place, which I am still discovering after seventeen years, is *like* Jesus Christ. In no way does it create the desire for license (which is freedom abused); rather, it creates the desire for less and less restriction of the inner-self, more and more willingness to learn to love, more and more longing for God himself. It causes one to breathe the very air of holy wonder, to despise the darkness, to run toward light. It is *like* Jesus Christ.

The wider place produces objectivity rather than subjectivity. I am not going about with my head in the clouds of new spirituality, shouting, "God has done a new work in *me*, hurray." I still speak only English and still dig for things out of the Bible just as always. My excitement over the wider place is not about me and my precious experience in it; it is about God. I have merely been freed to explore the wider place, to wander in it, to delight, to think with new liberty, to wonder as I have never wondered before at the greatness of God.

But where is the wider place?

It isn't a million light years away in some remote, distant plane of spiritual achievement. It is exclusively in no particular church, no doctrinal emphasis, no special religious technique, formula or dogma. It is not a result of ascetic disciplines. The potential of the wider place is in us all. Its location is everywhere. Paul had a way of communicating truth which no writer, to my knowledge, has ever matched. He wrote of the wider place: "Now the Lord is the Spirit, and where the Spirit of the Lord is, there is liberty—emancipation from bondage, freedom."

Emancipation from bondage means the door is wide open to more and more of life, to more and more maturity. Life means a *given* opportunity to grow. Being born merely means we have been set free to begin growing. Freedom without maturity is madness. Freedom without discipline can lead only to destruction. But this freedom, the freedom in the wider place of which we speak, *cannot* lead to madness or confusion as long as we realize that the wider place "is where the Spirit of the Lord is."

If the wider place is the place "where the Spirit of the Lord is," then nothing off-balance can come of our living in it. Jesus Christ defines the nature of God's Holy Spirit to us and he was the sanest person who ever walked our planet. The sanest and the most balanced. He didn't go overboard on any side issues; not baptism, not the Law, not even healing. At times he strode away from the crowds crushing in upon him for physical healing. Not because his heart lacked compassion for them; rather, I believe, because he wanted to avoid any appearance of imbalance, fanaticism. He sought no special spiritual thrill for himself. He of all persons, could have expounded at length on the inner joy he knew at being one with the Father. He could have eulogized the glories of heaven, using this as a gimmick to collect followers. He did none of this. He could not have been off-balance because his was the very nature of God. He remained free.

Jesus walked always in the wider place. He knew it well. It was not new to him. "In the beginning was the Word and the Word was with God and the Word was God." ". . . without him was not any thing made that was made." What may seem such a new discovery to us as dimly we begin to see the freedom of the wider place, was all known to him. None of us can know it on earth as he knew it. I doubt if we could cope with the knowing, even if it were possible.

But we can begin to live knowingly *in* the wider place *with* Jesus Christ. He is there to lead us about, to show us the wonders, to urge us toward more exploration. And if he is there, then we are safe from imbalance.

What is the key, then, to living in the wider place without fear of becoming swampy? Without fear of becoming what some would label heretical? I repeat, Paul has said it: "Now the Lord is the Spirit, and where the Spirit of the Lord is, there is liberty—emancipation from bondage, freedom."

But how do we know that what seems to us to be our wider place is not just that everything is going well in our lives for the moment? How do we differentiate between human joy and God's joy? How do we distinguish between the exhilaration of a great human love and the exhilaration of experiencing God's love? How do we know our "celestial times" with God are not merely psychological results of the joy of having turned a big deal or having written a good book, or of having found just the house we've always wanted? Certainly God rules out none of our human joy. But human joy comes so seldom and lasts such a short time, as a rule, it shouldn't confuse us deeply. God's joy goes right on when our hearts are breaking. God's joy has to do with laughter and happiness, but it also has to do with tears. It is not regulated by our circumstances. Our awareness of it can be dampened or heightened by what is currently happening to us, but nothing changes God's joy because nothing changes God.

One way, then to distinguish between mere human exhilaration and the discovery of God's wider place is the length of time each lasts, and its durability. God's joy is as eternal as God. God's joy is not altered by grief or persecution or disappointment or failure. We find the wider place with God *always there*. Our human "wider places" come and go.

There is another way to know whether our seeming wider place, our present sense of liberty is really of God. We have mentioned it already: the wider place that is of God is *like* Jesus Christ. Its environment produces results in our lives that cause us to *resemble him*. If we are living in the wider place of God-given freedom, we act like it.

If God permeates our wider place, we will find ourselves (surprisingly at times) living out the fruit of the Spirit of God himself. Paul also located the wider place—it is within us, where the Spirit of the Lord is. It has to do with inner-space, not outer-space. If we have come into God's wider place, we know it is within us; we don't fear disturbance from without and we show the signs. Do you remember the great Apostle's list of the signs of the Spirit of the Lord within us?

The first one is *love*. Love abounds in the wider place with God. Love so abounds in the wider place that we can know we're entering it, when we become increasingly aware that we are not loving enough. Unlove shows up at once in the wider place. If you can think of someone you don't love (aren't genuinely concerned for) and if you still feel "free in the spirit" and experience times of spiritual bliss, look the situation over carefully. The wider place with God encourages love, even toward those with whom we disagree, even toward those who misunderstand or persecute us. If the mention of someone's name curls your hair, look around you a bit more. The very atmosphere of the wider place is *love*. It is like Jesus, and although I'm sure he abhorred the evil in his enemies and found the jeering men at the foot of his cross unattractive, he went right on dying for them just the same. He had made it plain that if we are his, we are to love our enemies. He did not change under the pressure of the agony on the cross.

If the climate of your thinking is love, you are in the *safe* wider place. "He that loveth not knoweth not God; for God is love."

Paul mentions *joy* next as a direct result of the presence of the Spirit of God within us. He, of course, does not mean perpetual happiness, or the wearing of a never-relaxing grin on our faces, nothing artificial or assumed. He means joy. The joy Jesus said he was leaving with us. His own joy. The joy of God himself. "The Lord thy God . . . will joy over thee with singing." God is glad, is full of joy that we are alive. That he created us. We can't possibly understand this, but it has to be true.

Look around you in your wider place. If indestructible joy is there, God is there.

The next thing to look for in the wider place is *peace*. Is it peaceful where you are? Or do you have to be feverishly active from morning to night? Can you be content to be alone in your wider place with God? Even if you are at the moment, not experiencing his presence, can you be content to be alone with yourself? Or do you keep your date book full? Perhaps you are one of those who knows no inner peace because you are convinced that God has especially anointed you to save a certain number off what you consider the sinking ship of humanity. Can you spend a quiet, peaceful afternoon with a friend who is not of your doctrinal turn of mind? Or must you be everlastingly agitating to bring him over to seeing things your way? Do you feel an hour or a day of just walking through a light-filled woods a waste of time? Are you embroiled most of the time in some church trouble or other interpersonal relationship problem? True, we all have difficult personalities to cope with, but if *we* are acting in love and wisdom and forbearance, our wider place within us will be filled with peace. Do you carry a load of false guilt that keeps you on the defensive and is, by its very existence, an insult to the forgiving power of God?

Test the atmosphere of your inner place. Is there unpeace in it? If so, you are in the wrong place, but if you can get quiet, God has a surprise for you. "My peace I leave with you," Jesus said.

The next fruit listed as being there if the Spirit of the Lord is present is "patience, (an even temper, forbearance)." I, for one, lose touch with my wider place, my freedom, frequently here. My only progress report can come dated the day several years ago when I read somewhere that "impatience is lack of love." This pulls me up short. None of us goes through life or even through a day without some show of impatience. Particularly if we drive a car. Particularly if we see a lot of someone who makes a habit of being slow or of being late. Even if some of our reasons for being impatient are valid, according to the Bible, there is no excuse for indulging in it. And we lose ground rapidly if we berate ourselves as we go right on being impatient.

Impatience does not live long in the rarefied atmosphere of love in God's *safe* wider place.

The next sign that will determine if your wider place is of God is a check of your ability to be *kind*. How does your voice sound when you say hello the fourth time your telephone rings inside of twenty minutes? Certainly you have reason to be annoyed. But what about the unfortunate fourth caller? Does he or she deserve to be treated unkindly just because three other people dialed your number first? Believe me, I am not writing from a pinnacle here. During the time we are living in a rented beach cottage while our house is being built, I don't even have a telephone and I love every quiet, peaceful minute of it. But the chance to try *this* fruit of the Spirit (kindness) comes every time someone knocks on my door when I'm writing. So far, I have always found the fruit there. God never forgets one of his gifts for a single day. But if the habit of *drawing* on these gifts hadn't been formed, I'd be making some enemies. Can my neighbors here help it if I prefer not to have a telephone and if knocking on the door is the only way to reach me? The grocery boy, the clerk in the department store, even those who seem to high-hand you, are to receive kindness, according to God. Whether they deserve it is not the point. Do we deserve God's kindness? And didn't Jesus say the Father's kindness falls on the unjust as well as the just?

Kindness permeates the wider place with God.

Kindness and *goodness.* We all fail to make use of the gift of goodness from the Father. There is no totally good man or woman on earth. There has been only One and we crucified him. And yet he expects goodness of us. Some people we carelessly call "too good." I don't believe this for one minute. We tend to say this about overly-generous persons, persons who find it easy to smile, easy to give. Excessive generosity isn't necessarily a sign of goodness. Generous people can be "good people," but because I used to be overly-generous (and still have to watch it) I no longer see it as a bona fide virtue or sign of goodness. It can be a way to hide our insecurity, to buy our way into other people's affections. Only *goodness* as measured by the life of the Son of God is authentic. Some of us have a measure of natural goodness. Most of us are in scarce supply and so it is a glorious thing that we all have access to the goodness of the Spirit himself.

Faithfulness is the next sign in Paul's list. And it is so directly related to goodness as not to need much comment. Of course faithfulness, which comes as a gift from the Spirit of God, means faithfulness to him, but it also means faithfulness to each other. Have you ever speculated on how different all of life would be if more of us really practiced faithfulness to each other? Even though we vow we won't do it again, how quickly we jump to conclusions when we hear a smudge of gossip. We don't gossip often enough about the good things, you know. And in us all, in spite of our desire for it, is that lack of faithfulness which causes us to leap at every tidbit that can harm or tear down. I believe most of us *do* want to be faithful to our friends, to our loved ones, but why aren't we? Is it blind self-righteousness that causes us to betray people by gossip, or could it be that we are mainly seeking superiority or entertainment? Faithfulness implies commitment and only from the Spirit of God can we learn that. His commitment to us is total and it is forever. God's commitment to us is never altered by what we do or by what we leave undone.

Gentleness, the next fruit of the Spirit, will be everywhere in our wider place with God. The gentleness that springs from genuine meekness and humility. If we are humble, we never need to remind anyone of the fact. They will know it. Humility is not calling ourselves worms. Humility is possessing the almighty meekness and gentleness of God himself. A lady criticized me once for having called Jesus of Nazareth the greatest gentleman who ever lived. God bless her, I still think he was.

Gentleness will be there in your wider place, in your *safe* new freedom, if God is there. There is no humility to match the humility of God. And in his humility and his meekness and his gentleness we find all power and strength.

The last sign that God is present, according to Paul's list of the fruits of the Spirit which can, if we agree, show itself in our daily lives, is *self-control*. I wonder why Paul placed that last on his list? Someone once said it might be because it is the last of the fruits to come to us. I'd like to believe this in my weaker moments, but in all honesty, I cannot. When God comes, he brings all he is with him. He does not parcel things out. The Holy Spirit of God would not come to dwell in the believer and leave his self-control in heaven. I could never buy that. Our lack of self-control is simply due to the fact that we don't want it. And yet, with all my heart I believe it is one of the sure roads to complete inner-emancipation. Without self-control, we are bound emotionally, physically, socially, spiritually. The compulsive eaters, talkers, gossipers among us would do well to ask God to teach us to learn to love the freedom he offers in *self-control*. And have you noticed that the unbridled critical tongues and the overweight bodies frequently belong to the most ardent propagators of "separation" and "dedication?" Lack of self-control breeds chaos and unpeace within us and around us. Our wider place, if it is a *safe*, God-permeated wider place, brings us to love self-control. Shows us the freedom it brings. Gives us the strength to make use of the gift. Goethe was right when he wrote: "Whatever liberates our spirit without giving us self-control is disastrous."

The wider place, then, where the freedom of God is, is a *safe* place. The place of liberty where we breathe the native air of our origin in the Creator himself. It is, in a sense, an inner-Eden, to which we are permitted to return by grace. The wider place of which we speak is not a self-conjured super-spiritual Ivory Tower, shut away from the needs of our brothers. The wider place where God is, sharpens our sense of responsibility, whets eagerness within us for *real maturity*. It is not a closed-in sanctuary of escape. If your "wider place" is dependent upon your "spiritual" feelings, it is not of God. If it depends upon the measure of your service, it is not of God. Christians who weigh their worth to God solely by whether or not they are "serving" him in some noticeable way, are boxed in a corner, trapped. God never boxes us in a corner. The wider place where God is, does not close in, it opens out. After all, if there's room for God in the wider place, it *has* to be *big*. God will open out, will stretch, will heighten and deepen and expand our lives, as we learn to love his freedom.

". . . the Lord is the Spirit, and where the Spirit of the Lord is, there is liberty—emancipation from bondage, freedom."

WHAT IS FREEDOM?

If freedom is truth in action, and if Jesus Christ and God are one, then freedom in the life of any Christian must be simply God in action. God in action, freeing the human mind from the need to follow the herd, from the need to despise, from the need to prejudge, from the need to live inadequately, off balance.

3 / WHAT IS FREEDOM?

WHAT DOES IT MEAN TO BE "free indeed?" What is freedom?

Philosophically, it is truth in action. Socially, it is truth in action. Emotionally it is truth in action. Spiritually, it is truth in action.

Freedom, contrary to the popular concept, is *not* doing what we please when we please. Socially, emotionally, spiritually, this kind of abuse of freedom is the shortest road to slavery.

Freedom, according to the dictionary, is: "liberation from slavery, imprisonment or restraint. . . ." The definition of *liberty* enlarges the concept: "Liberty often differs from freedom in implying a power to say, do, what one wishes, as distinguished from being uninhibited in doing, thinking," etc.

Liberty, then, true liberty, is freedom fulfilled. If one has liberty, one has also the *power* to act in freedom.

This I believe to be the kind of freedom promised to the

followers of Jesus Christ. "And you will know the truth, and the truth will set you free." Words of Christ, further defining the premise that *freedom is truth in action.* The *truth* will set us free to *act.* It is not a matter of being naturally inhibited or uninhibited.

Can we know truth? Pilate asked this of the Man who stood before him, beaten, spit upon, tormented, enduring quietly the false trials, the long walks through the narrow, crooked streets of the Holy City, through the darkest night. "What is truth?" Pilate asked him. Apparently, Jesus answered nothing. We are told in John's account that Pilate "On saying this . . . went out to the Jews again and told them, I find no fault in Him."

Truth, Himself, stood before Pilate that night. There was no need for Him to answer the question in mere words. He, Himself, was the answer. He, Himself, was the truth. "I am the . . . truth."

If freedom is truth in action, and if Jesus Christ and God are one, then freedom in the life of any Christian must be simply God in action. God in action, freeing the human mind from the need to follow the herd, from the need to despise, from the need to prejudge, from the need to live inadequately, off balance.

I do not believe that God does this all at once. He works with the human mind and the human heart according to his knowledge of both. Never according to our knowledge. Only God's knowing is complete here. Only he could bear to know the human heart and still love, still act in its behalf, still care that it become ultimately free. This in no way, as I see it, minimizes or belittles the human intelligence. It merely clarifies God's intelligence and the capacity of his mind to know and his heart to love.

Human beings are not unimportant. Not to other human beings, certainly not to God. One of the most contradictory reactions in a Christian is to belittle himself, to denegate his worth, to confuse humility with self-depreciation. We are of the utmost importance to God. If we are not, then he really took part in a ridiculously unnecessary effort when he came to this earth and lived and died so that we earth-people could come to understand something of his nature, his intentions toward us. If we are not of the highest importance to God, then he took part in a gigantic waste of divine energy, both in his creation and his redemption of human life.

Philosophically, then, freedom is truth in action: God in action in behalf of our release from all that binds us, from all that makes us stupid, insensitive; from all that makes us mimics, erratic half-doers, living only on the surface and in the margins of life.

"If the Son therefore shall make you free, ye shall be free indeed." Is this true *socially?* Is freedom to live in harmony with our fellow human beings, to get along with the members of our families, the other people in our churches, our fellow workers—is this kind of freedom God in action? If it is, then why don't we do a better job of it? Why do so many churches give such good ammunition to the non-believer? My brother was slow to come to an authentic belief in Jesus Christ. I do not see this as his fault entirely. He is a realist. He is basically an honest man. For most of his life he has had contact with a few well-meaning, but quite unfree Christians, who have urged and urged that he come to like to go to church. He has gone, most of the time, more or less to keep the peace, as my father did, before his personal experience with Jesus Christ late in his life. But I think I will never forget one evaluation of a certain church my brother made in a rebellious mood many years ago: "There's only one recommendation I'd make to those people. They should have an usher stationed out front, to see that the congregation checks its firearms at the door." The usual battle had been raging. My brother is not a fighter. By nature, he is outgoing and gets along well with almost any kind of person. This remark was not as uncalled for as the "good" stunned church folk thought. To me, and I'm certain, to God, it just revealed my brother's inner longing. His heart *wanted* the fighting not to be true. His heart *wanted* to find harmony, the kind of love God's people are supposed to have, plain down-to-earth friendliness—people living up to what they so stoutly professed to believe. He wanted some honesty. Some freedom to be himself along his own particular pilgrimage toward God. He resisted quarreling, gossiping insensitive people who tried to hurry him unnaturally along his way toward the Christian life.

I resisted them too. I hope I always shall, because Jesus did when he was on earth. "Let him who is without sin among you be the first to throw a stone at her!" he shouted, as the self-righteous Pharisees took up stones to kill the woman caught in the act of adultery. *They* followed certain rules and they followed them so proudly, their hearts were twisted out of shape, their capacities to love, to care, cramped and bound. Jesus did not step according to their rules and they crucified him. But this did not rid them of his caring. Just as nothing can rid us of the love of God—nothing can separate a human heart from his heart, so murdering the Son of God on a cross did not rid the rule-followers of his pursuit—even of them. Jesus got up out of the tomb and walks today, toward every human heart, offering the same freedom he offered to the pompous, fat-bellied, silk-robed religious little men who engineered his death and stood sneering beneath his cross.

Yes, this God is big enough to give harmonious social freedom to us all. To the pagan who despises bigoted churchgoers, to the self-righteous church-goer who despises the pagan bigot. He is even big enough and loving enough and persistent enough to give the freedom to work together amicably to every member of every church committee in all of Christendom! That we have only partially taken this emancipation is an insult to God. More than that, it is the cause of his greatest heartbreak, as I see it. It must be. Church-goers have at least been exposed to some of God's nature. They have heard the Scriptures read on Christmas and on Easter. They are not unaware that Jesus Christ loved the world enough to come and be a part of it for as long as those he loved permitted him to stay alive. They are not unaware of the fact that he did get up out of his tomb and lives today in the closing years of the twentieth century. They have heard this, and so fighting, headstrong, critical Christians must be a heartbreak to God—a heartbreak so vast and so steady, we couldn't comprehend it. If God loves as we know him to love, then he must grieve proportionately.

Does God offer freedom in family relationships too? If he did not, wouldn't he be a fiend? Aren't families, marriages, births, homes all God's idea? Didn't he start it all in the first place? And being God, wouldn't he long to assume responsibility for these families? I have written at length on this in other books,* but the very subject of family relationships moves us smoothly to the next way in which God is in action toward us to free us: *emotionally.* Most family problems are due to flailing, out-of-control emotions. Plain old emotional immaturity on someone's part—perhaps on the part of each person involved in the fracas.

Would more freedom of the kind the Son promised help untangle our troubles among our relatives and immediate families? Think about it. One of the strongest characteristics of emotional freedom, one of the surest signs of emotional maturity is *balance.* Just imagine what might happen if even one person in a troubled family had balance. If just one person could accept the other members *as they are* without making a personal issue of everything. A friend called once to weep into our ears because her husband of a few years had forgotten their wedding anniversary. She was completely crushed, dead certain he didn't love her any more, sure their marriage was going on the rocks. He just forgot, that's all. He was simply busy and forgot. My beloved father did not remember his wedding anniversary once without a reminder in forty-three years of married life. Mother laughed about it and declared she didn't marry him so that he would remember the date on which the happy event took place. She married

* *What Is God Like? Woman to Woman. Woman's Choice.*

him because she loved him. She kept her love for him in focus, in balance, and accepted him as he was—forgetful, among other things. But she didn't take it as a personal insult to her. She kept her balance. And only laughter and more joking about his absent-mindedness resulted. He was not made to feel like an ungrateful, unloving wretch. He was made to feel free. And of course, mother was free of self-pity, and my brother Joe and I were free of having to live through a family quarrel.

I am only beginning to see the freedom that would result—freedom in family and community life, in political life, in the affairs of nations—if only there were more emotional maturity. Not being a psychologist I back away from mere theory or academic answers. But I do see the unfolding truth, and what I see at this point is that if only a few of us would accept the gift of emotional freedom God holds out to us daily, we could change history around us. One emotionally balanced person can keep the peace. One person willing to be misunderstood without fighting back, can keep the peace. This is a difficult lesson to learn—to be willing to be *misunderstood*. But freedom results, not only for us, it can result eventually for the one who misunderstands us. Our human tendency when we know ourselves to be misunderstood is to work away at it, to try to get things straight, even to acting dishonestly in order to assuage or pacify the other person. This is not Christian. Jesus Christ did not defend himself, and if anyone on earth ever had reason to, he did. "He came unto his own and his own received him not." Not only did they disagree with Jesus, not only did they misunderstand his every motive, they plotted to get rid of him. Or tried to. They didn't bring it off. He is still here, offering his gift of freedom from misunderstanding, from being misunderstood. We are going to be misunderstood. No one escapes it. Of course, we should try to keep our motives clear, try not to be neglectful, forgetful, careless, but no one will make it one hundred percent on this earth. So, why don't we take his gift of freedom here? Why do we go on battling for complete understanding, especially from those we love most, when complete understanding is just not possible among human beings? God said, "I *am* understanding." He is. But only he is.

What is *spiritual* freedom? If God offers philosophical, emotional and social freedom—if he is truth in action to give us these freedoms, doesn't it stand to reason that he also offers spiritual freedom? What is it? Perhaps our problem lies here. Is it freedom to follow any old doctrine or the ideas and concepts of anyone who happens to get a publisher to bring out his book? Is it freedom to be swayed by the thoughts and expressed ideas of anyone who manages to stand on a platform with a captive audience before him? Obviously not. It seems to me, spiritual freedom is the state of having become childlike with God. Not childish, childlike. Jesus said that unless or until we become as little children we could not possibly understand the kingdom of God. Could not possibly enter into the freedom he offers to everyone. It is never that God's willingness to give is in question; it is always our unwillingness to receive. We get all set with our favorite doctrine, snuggled down into the highly-organized folds of our favorite denomination, work our heads off at what we call service to God, and the airless place around us grows stuffier by the day. On Sunday morning our ministers thank God in their pastoral prayers that "we are free to come to this place of worship." They should thank him. We are free physically and legally to go to the church of our choice. Our government does not prohibit it. Most of us have long cars in which to ride. No one is stopping us from going. But what about the shriveling of our over-regulated spirits? The ever shrinking walls of our souls? The subtle closing in —perhaps closing *down* of our minds?

I once spoke at a specially called early evening meeting in a church of an enormous denomination. After I finished, the ladies from that church, who had been energetic enough to call the meeting so that I could be there, walked me across the downtown square enabling me to keep another speaking date already scheduled at another church of a not quite so enormous denomination. The ladies from the first church had been so warm toward me, so complimentary, declaring they had been counting the days until I was to be at *their* church, that I naturally assumed they were going to accompany me into the second church to hear me speak again. My ego took a big tumble. And my seeing enlarged. They were so conditioned to their own snug harbor, they hadn't even thought of attending the second church! It wasn't their denomination.

Now, to interpret anything here as advocating disloyalty to one's own church, is to miss the point entirely. Most certainly I don't recommend becoming a church tramp, but I do recommend taking the gift of God's freedom for your spirit. After all, this particular gift goes far beyond the rather superficial custom of *having*, absolutely having to attend every service of any one church. It goes all the way into *you*. It goes all the way into *me*. It frees us from meaningless conformity. I remember my father saying once of a friend: "Oh, the way he's fixed up with God, he's free to worship anywhere."

True spiritual freedom involves the inner man, the inner woman. How to achieve it? There is no quick, painless way, and it is *not* an achievement. It is a gift. A gift which most of us are merely in the process of learning to receive. It is ready for us, prepared before the foundation of the world, as the Lamb was. But God, being God, must first be able to trust us with it. Anyone who deliberately sets out to find spiritual freedom can become swampy, can lose his Christian definition. Freedom is not something we find. It is something God gives, not all at once in a package. He gives freedom as he knows we are ready to handle it, to make creative use of it, not to twist it to license. And God is never early and never late.

WHO NEEDS MORE FREEDOM?

God looks on the inner man to find him in need of liberty and then he begins his loving pursuit of the man to set him free in all areas of life. Free to think clearly, free to live abundantly, free to identify with the lowest among us without lowering his own standards, free to be proven wrong, free to be mistreated and misunderstood without rancor and self-pity. Free to learn, however gradually, the art of living day and night in the wider place. The place God has prepared for us right on this earth.

4 / WHO NEEDS MORE FREEDOM?

JESUS SELDOM HAD a chance to say all he planned to say without interruption of some kind. His words were so revolutionary, so new, so strange to the devoutly religious men of his day, it seems, according to the Scriptural accounts, that he managed only a sentence or two at a time before someone interrupted him. Before someone began to disagree with him, to question his authority, his right to speak. After all, few of them believed Jesus was the Son of God. Perhaps no one realized it clearly enough to have put it into words.

And so, as he stood teaching before a motley crowd of believers in the court of the Temple in Jerusalem one day, the argument began, much as all the others had begun, following a statement from Jesus which shocked his listeners:

". . . If you abide in My Word—hold fast to My teachings *and* live in accordance with them—you are truly My disciples. And," he added, "you will know the truth and the truth will set you free."

Suddenly the crowd began to jostle and murmur and some of the more opinionated among them shouted: "We are Abraham's offspring (descendants) and have never been in bondage to anybody. What do You mean by saying, You will be set free?"

And the argument was under way. Why? Did these people feel superior? They were descendants of Abraham, the man through whom God had begun their nation. Theirs was a proud heritage. To them the proudest. The most to be desired of any heritage known to man. For Jesus to infer that *they*, the sons of Abraham, were in bondage to any-one or anything, struck a nerve, and they struck back at him. How dare he infer that they needed more freedom? They were of the race of God's chosen people. They were the children of Israel. Didn't this make them favored of God? In fact, to their circumspect, conditioned minds Jesus was challenging the Lord God himself by his audacious infer-ence that *they* needed freedom. They needed nothing. They were Israelites, the sons of Abraham. "We . . . have never been in bondage to anybody."

Too many of us are like the irate people in Jesus' audience that day: haughty, proud, self-contained, safe in our human heritages, unaware of our desperate need. Hemmed about by genealogies and huge oil portraits of our ancestors, gazing down on the less fortunate with the same imperturbable stares with which our painted antecedents gaze down upon us as we wander through the airless rooms of our daily lives. We don't have to be materially wealthy to hold on to our family pride, to settle for a genteel, traditional nod in God's direction on Sunday morning because "of course our family has always attended worship." We need not even have an old oil painting of our particular familiar patriarch around the house. We need not live in a mansion as such. We can strut through our narrow days in exactly the same prison of family security if the whole fortune has been long lost or never existed in the first place. And perhaps the saddest aspect of it all is that most of us do not know we are in bondage, do not know we need to be set free from anything. Our respectable suburbs and high-rise apartments and shaded, small town "best" houses are peopled with well-meaning, sincere, even appealing men and women who *feel* as free as the breeze through the tall trees on a summer evening . . . unaware of the bondage, satisfied, pathetically—even humorously closed away from reality. Their ears so stopped by self-preoccupation with their own worth they do not hear the truth of the words that are spoken to them; only what they want to hear.

In a book of Georgia tall tales there is the story of a little old lady who attended a lecture at her church. The visiting speaker's topic centered around the history and the activities of the ancient Medes and the Persians of Biblical times. The man worked his way through the talk, making his points with care and precision, tying up his conclusions in a neat bundle, and sat down. At the church door when the lecture was over, he stood greeting the members of his audience, accepting their thanks, their comments, feeling he had been a success. *Until* our little old lady minced toward him, a smile wreathing her daintily wrinkled face, her hand outstretched. "Oh, Dr. So and So," she drawled in her aristocratic Georgian manner, "I did so enjoy that talk. You know my *mother* was a Mead!"

My mother was a Mead.

We are Abraham's descendants.

We don't need to be let out of slavery. We have never bowed our necks to anyone! That, of course, is our trouble. The cause of our blindness. The heavy bolt on the door that keeps out the clear light of freedom.

As long as the sons of Abraham clung to their heritage, even Jesus Christ could do little for them. They were called his followers. They called themselves that. But he knew what was in man. All men, including those who professed to be his disciples. He knew their need of freedom.

He still knows what is in all men, even those among us who proclaim from the housetops that we are his followers. And he sees us in our pathetic need of a wider place in which to function. Sees us, blessedly, through the eyes of love and indestructible caring about our imprisonment.

Sees us through the eyes of love? Yes. But with a very different meaning from the one we usually give that cliché. God's love corrects, untangles, straightens out, opens the windows, lets in the light—frees.

Of all men on earth, Jesus Christ was not a legalist, I can find not one touch of the static in his words: They are life, with the movement of life, always opening outward, even when they appear to our imprisoned minds and our blinded eyes to be confining us. He never spoke in trite formulas. Jesus Christ always spoke in fresh realities. He knew what was in man, so he did not expect man to act or to react in a way of which man was not capable. I see nothing in Jesus' teaching or in his conduct that indicates that to become his follower one must lose his personality and become a carbon copy of anyone else. I see nothing in any of his ideas that propagates conformity for conformity's sake. Conformity hems in. Christian faith opens out. Christian faith makes room for originality and imagination. It does not produce conformity and legalism. It is not a hothouse for inflexible minds. True, some of the most static-minded human beings on earth flock together like plaster images of each other proclaiming themselves to be Christians. No one should (or if he is truly Christian no one *could*) challenge the work God has done in their eternal souls. But wherever we spot inflexibility, legalism, the static mind, we are not seeing true Christianity lived out in the freedom Jesus Christ offers. What we are saying here has nothing to do with *which* doctrine you clutch for dear life, nor has it anything to do with *which* passage of Scripture you swear by—it has only to do with God's crying need for *free* followers. Followers who do not need to show discourtesy if someone is behaving in a way *they* disapprove. Followers who are free enough to be ladies and gentlemen at *all* times, no matter where they find themselves. Followers who are inclusive, never exclusive.

I hadn't thought of this misguided lady in years, but just

now she flashed into my mind: I was in a dining car on a speeding train going to Oregon. The car was, perhaps, half-full of business men, couples, ladies alone, like myself, teen-agers—the usual assortment of travelers. And into the car lurched a portly lady in her sixties. Half-way down the aisle, she heaved into my table, ramming her thumb into my cup of coffee, then hit the table across the aisle, upsetting a gentleman's martini. She smiled at first, and started to apologize, embarrassed. The gentleman got up quickly, wiped the lady's coat sleeve where some of his drink had splattered, and was just about to assure her it was all right, that he knew it was an accident, when she pulled herself up to her full height and said quite audibly: "Oh, me. I was going to say I'm sorry. But now that I see what I spilled—Humph." She turned to leave, mumbling that this was no fit place for a Christian to eat!

Perhaps I should say in passing, that her appetite got the better of her later. I sat for an hour or so over my coffee, and in a little while, she reappeared, looked all around, saw no one with a drink, sat down and ate heartily.

It's quite possible she thought she had witnessed to Jesus Christ from behind her self-satisfied wall; I don't know. I was relieved that she did not sit down at my table or even near enough to start a conversation. Women like this one make me feel guilty just for being alive, if I forget to think through to God's viewpoint and see them as they are—pitiable behind their prison walls, desperately in need of his kind of freedom. His kind of freedom from rudeness, from self-satisfaction, from pride in one's own kind. What if Jesus had been like that self-righteous woman? Would he ever have reached Mary Magdalene? Would he ever have reached Levi? Would he ever have reached me?

Jesus did not pick out an assortment of prohibitions for us which didn't happen to appeal to him, you know. Isn't it just possible that he is as opposed to excessive eating as to excessive wine-bibbing? Or excessive *anything* for that matter. God is balanced. He is free. God looks on the inner man to find him in need of liberty and then he begins his loving pursuit of the man to set him free in all areas of life. Free to think clearly, free to live abundantly, free to identify with the lowest among us without lowering his own standards, free to be proven wrong, free to be mistreated and misunderstood without rancor and self-pity. Free to learn, however gradually, the art of living day and night in the wider place. The place God has prepared for us right on this earth.

Who needs more freedom? We all need it. As much as those self-righteous sons of Abraham who shouted at Jesus in the Temple court that day. In his perceptive reply to them lies the secret of recognizing our need for freedom: "Jesus answered them, I assure you, most solemnly I tell you, Whoever commits and practices sin is the *slave* of sin."

Do we practice no sin? Not even sins of attitude? Is there not one gossip among us? Not one glutton? Not one prejudiced mind? Not one who leans on his own heritage? His own judgment? Is there no liar anywhere in Christendom? No one who takes the easy way of flattery instead of honesty? No income tax dodgers? No materialists? No one who would find Christianity not so palatable if he didn't own his own home and have obedient children? No one who would praise God a little less if his business dropped off next year?

We all sin. We all practice sin. But this is not a book about sin. It is about freedom from sin which can grow *in* us as a gift from God, when we come to love his freedom enough.

PART II

The Spirit of the Lord [is] upon Me, because He has
anointed Me [the Anointed One, the Messiah] to preach
the good news (the Gospel) to the poor; He has sent Me
to announce release to the captives, and recovery of
sight to the blind; to send forth delivered those who are
oppressed—who are downtrodden, bruised, crushed
and broken down by calamity.

Luke 4:18 (The Amplified Bible)

FREEDOM FROM CONFUSION ABOUT GOD

God is not the author of confusion. He is, in Jesus Christ, the Light of the World, the clarification of man's perplexities. This is the liberating news he came to bring us.

5 / FREEDOM FROM CONFUSION ABOUT GOD

JESUS CHRIST DECLARED himself to be the Anointed One sent from God. This was either true or it was not true. Christians stake their daily and eternal lives on its being true. It was on this truth that my own life changed its course, was turned completely around to face the other way. There was no fear of Dante's inferno in me. Nor was there a longing for heaven—at least not consciously. I was merely another materialistic western-world pagan, with potentially good instincts and already proven bad ones. God had no reality, no meaning, no place in my life. I had long since stopped berating him, had settled restlessly, but definitely into the sometimes dull, sometimes exciting pursuit of my own happiness, my own pleasure, my own success. Many things went wrong, the problems piled up, but until I was thirty-three years of age, I managed to wiggle through the tight places with the financial help of my parents, and on my own one point of comfort: Nothing is permanent but change. If things stacked up on me, I just went on, tried to ignore them or bluff my way out, consoling myself at night when I was alone with my pillow, that no matter how tangled up things seemed at the moment, since nothing was permanent but change, the problems, too, would somehow resolve themselves or just go away. It never occurred to me to pray. I knew my mother prayed and some of my Roman Catholic friends attended Mass regularly, but God had no conscious place in my life whatever.

At the age of thirty-three, almost on a dare, I began to believe that God was *knowable*. That he need not be formless, vague, remote, a mere subject for discussion or heated argument, a pacifier for old ladies, a policeman for little children. I began to believe this so all inclusively that I turned my life over to him. "My life" included all there was of me. It included my pursuit of pleasure, my work, my friends, my good and bad habits, my viewpoint, my rights to myself and my heart.

You can be very sure that I did not make this commitment to an amorphous, vague, remote Creature whom man called God. My commitment came as a direct result of the discovery of truth. The truth that Jesus Christ and God are one and the same, that if I could know Jesus Christ, I could know God. In that sense Jesus Christ redeemed God for me. I had no trust in the God of my mother or my friends. I didn't *know* him. I saw no way to know God. When someone claimed to know him, it sounded pompous to me, or infantile, or unintelligent, superstitious. I remember arguing many years before that I might trust God if he were knowable, but I certainly would take no mere human word for his existence. I saw no remote possibility that any human being could know God, and so I did not believe he existed in any practical way.

How then did I manage to come to the place of giving God the most important gift I owned—myself? After reading the opening verses of the first chapter of John, I took the one leap of faith required to know God. I tossed aside my mental blocks and *believed* that Jesus Christ was not just the leader of one religious movement. That he spoke the truth when he declared himself to *be* the truth about God. When he claimed to be one with the Father. It was as simple as that. So simple, it is the most difficult act for complex man to perform.

I suppose it is rather obvious why we demand explanations where God is concerned. We believe our astronauts are in space, doing what they report they're doing, although not one in ten thousand of us understands one thing about the science of outer space. We believe anything science brings into being, but we demand to know the intricate "whys" of God. We do this, of course, because it requires nothing of us but some tax dollars to believe what happens in outer space. When we believe God, if our faith is real, it will begin to involve our very lives. Even those who proclaim *no faith* as adamantly as I proclaimed it, hold far down in their hearts a secret knowledge that if they come to believe, God is going to change their way of living, their attitudes, their minds, their hearts. He will, if we give him half a chance. He could not remain true to himself or to his love for us if he didn't. He does not turn us into duplicates of each other, but he works steadily and loves constantly until bit by bit what is destructive in our natures is changed.

It is cruel, in my opinion, to urge any human being toward an encounter with Jesus Christ glibly promising success in business, a happy home life, no more problems. Usually, the conflicts increase when one has turned to Christ. There are then the shocks of seeing oneself for the first time as one really is—desperately in continuous need of a Savior. We bring him at conversion what we thought were our big problems, and find that they were not the big ones at all. The big ones lie hidden deep within us, in our attitudes of heart, our thought patterns formed in self-defense, our prejudices, our doubts.

But this is not a dissertation on the tribulations of the new

Christian. The intention is merely to emphasize the fact that there is only one safe ground on which to give one's life to God: the single fact of the *identity* of Jesus Christ. God can appear to be a white-whiskered, sentimental grandfather if a human heart turns to him merely to get out of his or her own current troubles. And this concept of God is as far off as a concept could possibly be. There is only one safe point on which to make the turning: Jesus Christ and God are one and the same. Jesus of Nazareth was God, come at last to live with us in the mainstream of human history. No one can, and no one ever will be able to explain that. Here is the one place—*the one place* where blind faith is required. With some, reaching this place is a slow, painful process. With me, it happened to be almost immediate. I had always admired the character and manhood of Jesus of Nazareth above any other figure in human history. This is how he redeemed God for me. If God is like Jesus of Nazareth— if, still more pertinent, Jesus of Nazareth came to reveal God in all his fullness, then this God I can trust. He was then, not a remote God, dwelling "on high," far removed from the hatred and murderous madness of our earth. He had come to earth to get in it all *with us*. Within the first clarified moments of my new faith, I thought of the burned, blackened bodies of my fellow human beings who happened to be unfortunate enough to have lived in either Nagasaki or Hiroshima, Japan. The only release I had found for my own heart's devastation when we dropped the bombs on those hapless people, was to scoff at anyone who believed there could be a God who cared about humanity.

Then Jesus Christ became God to me.

And I understood why Christians believed in a loving God. I still didn't understand the suffering of the world, no one ever will, but I understood that God was not remote from it, was not impervious to it, was not just standing there by his comfortable golden throne doing nothing. He had already done something. He had *already come here* in an equally bloody era in human history (they don't change, really, these bloody eras; we merely have more people to destroy now and more efficient means). God had come *to us* and had not only lived out his earthly life healing and blessing and teaching, he had entered right into the black, evil, painful depths of human suffering on his own cross. I had fought the injustice of unmerited suffering such as the suffering my own country's bombs had inflicted upon those women and children and old men in Japan, none of whom had been involved in Pearl Harbor. But was there ever a more blameless person murdered since time began to be counted than Jesus Christ, the Son of God?

This did not change the slaughter at Hiroshima or Manassas or Iwo Jima, but it did bring God into it for me. Is it any wonder that Jesus Christ called himself the very Light of the World?

A few hours before I began writing this chapter, I received a telegram telling me of the death of a friend—a vital, thoroughly Christian man in his forties, Russ Guder, whose wife Eileen Guder's book, *We're Never Alone*, is to me, one of the most important books published in 1965. Russ died of leukemia, as my own father did. Russ was my friend, and I treasure his letter written a few weeks before he died in which he said: "My faith is strong, quiet and experienced, Genie. Like Pope John, my 'bags are packed and ready.'" Still we prayed fervently for his healing, trying, all of us, to believe that God would heal Russ and yet wanting God's will. Russ improved amazingly, and then he died. I loved him, so I rejoice for *him*. But what about Eileen, who loved her husband with all her being? I know she will go on being God's woman for the rest of her lonely life on earth. Her faith, too, "is strong, quiet and experienced." But her life here is forever maimed. Russ is gone. He will not come back. Eileen is my friend too, and I grieve with her, but she will make creative, redemptive use of her loss and her heartbreak. When she has passed through the first bad days of attempting to learn how just to do the daily things without Russ, she will begin to allow God to make use of her tragedy. She will

write another book some day and it will be an even more
important one. But Eileen Guder is an authentic Christian.
She has lived her daily life with Jesus Christ for years now.
She won't have to grab wildly for comfort from a God she
doesn't know. She knows him and knows him to be trustworthy—worthy of her trust. She can, through her tears,
even during the most helpless moments of grief and loneliness,
turn with confidence to him. How could she do this—how
could any man or woman do this unless he or she *knew* the
Person toward whom the turning is made? One can *know*
God only in Jesus Christ. Jesus Christ, the Anointed One of
God, the Messiah—the God-Man, who came to live among
us in our sorrow, our grief, our hostility. Jesus Christ, the
Messiah, who came to bear our griefs and carry our sorrows.
The very Son of God, no *less* than God, who came to expose
himself to our hatred, our vengeance, our panic—this God is
knowable.

We cannot find our way safely to the wider place, where
the Spirit of this God is, unless we are aware of him as he
really is.

There is little or no freedom for the Christian who dwells
on God's vengeance, who conforms for the sake of conformity, who has never seen the heart of the Nazarene who
healed on the Sabbath and spoke meaningfully to a despised
Samaritan woman. There is no freedom for the tense,
shackled Christian who thinks exclusively—shutting out one
race, or one social background, or who insists upon bending
others to his own legalistic approach to God. Human beings
don't approach God anyway! God approaches human beings.
And his heart is all *inclusive*. He never shuts out. His arms
stretched wide on the cross of Calvary are his concentrated
demonstration of the welcoming nature of his love.

To live safely in the wider place, where freedom is, one
must be acutely aware of the *nature* of the Spirit of the Lord
who dwells there too. God is not on the side of conservative
or liberal, of enemy or ally. He is on everyone's side. There
is no cheering in heaven when the reports come in that six

hundred "enemy" troops have been killed in Viet Nam.
He loved every Viet Cong who fell. Loved him as much
as he loves you, or your son if he is fighting there. God loves
the parents or wives of the men who will not die, just as much
as he loves you, if your son or husband has died in Viet Nam.

We can have no pat explanation for tragedy. Only the
shallow mind would try for one. But we do have an explanation of God's nature—of God himself, in Jesus Christ. Sin is
loose in the world, war is, but it is not God's idea. Leukemia
is not God's idea. Creation is somehow incomplete. The cure
for leukemia will be found. Not soon enough to keep my
father here to fill my mother's life, nor to keep Russ Guder
beside Eileen, but this in no way changes Jesus Christ. He
did not call the ten legions of angels to save himself, either.
If he had, he wouldn't dare try to comfort a grief-stricken
human heart.

Jesus Christ does dare, though, because he has expended
every effort—just think, *every* effort known to God, to make
himself knowable to us. To blot out once and for all, the
confusion rampant in the human race about the true nature
of the Creator God. Every effort? Yes. God came, himself,
in the person of Jesus of Nazareth. There need never be confusion about him again. Our confusion stems from trying to
understand God through circumstances, through our griefs
and our joys. If your life is full of good things as you read
this, then God is a good God to you. But what about Eileen
Guder today in her fresh grief? Is God a good God to her?
Yes, he is, because she knows him in Jesus Christ.

There are times when it is as important to be sure that
God is an *involved* God, as well as a good God, and in
Jesus Christ, no one could doubt the divine involvement. He
is involved with us and he is committed to us. God never
gives up on a human heart. God's total explanation of himself to man *is* the Anointed One of God, the Messiah, Jesus
Christ.

Our questions are not necessarily answered in words or
theories, they are blotted out in the light of Jesus' involve-

ment, his goodness, his commitment, his love. The love that poured from the heart men tore open on Calvary.

God is not the author of confusion. He is, in Jesus Christ, the Light of the world, the clarification of man's perplexities. This is the liberating news he came to bring us.

FREEDOM FOR WHOM?

God backs up any search for freedom, but he can only give his liberty to those who have received him. It isn't that he doesn't want everyone to be free. It is merely that he *cannot* give his gifts to a human being who is closed to him. It is never God who withholds a gift. It is always man who refuses it. God does back up our search for freedom, but he can only give freedom to his followers, and then only to those who have learned to love it enough to make use of it.

6 / FREEDOM FOR WHOM?

E VERYONE NEEDS MORE FREEDOM and everyone has a right to it, because every human being on earth was created by the One who declared that if He made a man free, he would be free indeed. If God had not believed in human freedom, he would not have created us with the ability to make choices. If he had wanted a planet populated with puppets, he would have created a planet populated with puppets. God is squarely behind the pursuit of freedom from any real bondage for every person. It should surprise no one that the propagators of Communism are atheistic. God and bondage just do not go together.

Everyone on earth needs more freedom of one kind or another, although the fortunate, those of us who live in America, for example, mainly need freedom in our inner lives. I hear intelligent Americans complain bitterly about how we are "losing our liberties" in this country. This never fails to surprise me. I have never been so grateful to be an American as I am right now. I have never been so aware of my own freedom—never so grateful to awaken every morning remembering that I am God's child and an American citizen. Perhaps this gratitude stems from a new awareness of the bondage in much of the rest of the world. Whatever the cause, I am grateful for what I consider to be, for me, more practical daily freedom to live as I choose than can be found anywhere else on this earth. Americans do not inhabit a perfect land with a flawless, all-wise government, but with all our weaknesses and foibles, we are *free* to move ahead in the world struggle for freedom for every man. We are free to be free. Can anyone ask more than that? I, along with you, wish I didn't have to pay so much federal income tax. And now that I live in Georgia, I will also pay a state income tax, and a much higher property tax than I paid in Illinois. But the only thing that concerns me about my taxes in America is scraping up the money to pay them. How immature would I be to complain about increased taxes in my newly adopted state? I was *free* to make my own decision to move to Georgia, wasn't I? My haphazard assortment of belongings was not inspected, I needed no special government permit —I just moved becaused I wanted to move.

Every citizen of America, of course, has not always had full freedom as I have had by the mere accident of having been born white. But this is changing, thank God, and one day I expect to see, in my own lifetime, freedom for all American citizens to live up to their talents and their capabilities and their dreams.

While some of us are free in the ways others are not, the need is equal in us all for *inner freedom*: the quality of inner freedom Jesus promised to all those who *love* it enough to accept it as a gift from him. His gifts never wear out. If he gives something, it is eternal in its quality. It doesn't tarnish or rust or rub thin or wash away. We tend to act as though his gifts are not particularly lasting but it is our willingness to accept and make use of them that wears out. Never the gifts.

Can every human being on earth be truly free in his inner

self? Yes. It isn't at all likely that every human being will learn how to receive that freedom, but it is possible, or Jesus Christ was wrong when he declared: "If the Son therefore shall make you free, ye shall be free indeed."

Did he mean this only for his followers? The Scriptural setting for that verse as written by John in his gospel, indicates that Jesus was speaking to those who had chosen to believe in him, to follow him. But I see nothing in God's written down Word that tells us Jesus excluded anyone in any promise he made. The point to remember here is that *only* his followers can fully receive this freedom he promises. Only his followers, empowered by his Holy Spirit, can learn how to make use of it. God backs up any search for freedom, but he can only give his liberty to those who have received him. It isn't that he doesn't want everyone to be free. It is merely that he *cannot* give his gifts to a human being who is closed to him. It is never God who withholds a gift. It is always man who refuses it. God does back up our search for freedom, but he can only give freedom to his followers, and then only to those who have learned to love it enough to make use of it. After all, only those who have received him, have any notion that he made the offer in the first place.

Anyone can know the freedom Jesus Christ claimed to give, but it would not only be impossible for him to give it, it would be impossible for those who do not believe in him ever to learn to use his kind of liberty. Learning to make use of the liberty God gives must be done under the guidance of the Holy Spirit. It must be learned under his guidance, and *power* and *restraint* are required before we can begin to make use of it. When Christ offers freedom, he is not merely offering human freedom, civil rights—the freedom that guarantees that every man share the freedom of every other man. He offers the freedom characteristic only of God himself.

In a very real sense, then, God can safely offer freedom only to his own. But the overpowering intention of his heart has always been and always will be that every person in the world is welcome where he is concerned. God has not chosen a select few. He has chosen us all to grow into the full stature of sons of God. The offer has already been made. Redemption is an accomplished fact, and it is available and waiting for anyone who will claim it by faith in Jesus Christ, the Son. God's arms are open. "Come unto me, *all* ... ," Jesus said. "Behold, I stand at the door, and knock; if *any* man hear my voice, and open the door, I will come in. . . ." This includes you and it also includes your enemies; it includes the politicians whose very names mentioned on a newscast snap your heart shut; it includes Communist Russia and Communist China and all their satellites and all the free world. God knows no political barriers, no national barriers. "The middle wall of partition has been broken down. . . ."

God has no prejudices. He is free and he offers *his kind* of freedom to us all. One simple, awesome step of faith is all that is required to put us on our way to receiving his freedom: the simple, childlike placing of our trust in Jesus Christ. Not the determined effort to find a stimulating, exciting "moment of crisis." Not a demand from God that one *feel* the freedom at once. We are all different and if we had a set pattern for conversion to Jesus Christ, it would be deadening.

At the time of my own conversion, I merely looked at the friend with me and told her I guessed she was right about God, and I was wrong. She had loyally claimed throughout our discussions that God and Jesus Christ were one. I began to agree with her and God reached me. C. S. Lewis, one of Christendom's most effective apologists, was converted to God first, then Jesus Christ became real to him. Mrs. Billy Graham doesn't remember the time of her conversion at all. She was too young, but who can doubt it?

God demands no set procedure. We are told in the Bible that he looks on the heart. And so anyone, just anyone who wants God's freedom enough can have it.

If this is true, then why are there so many bound up

Christians? Why did Jesus feel it expedient to declare in the presence of his followers that if he set a man free, he would be free indeed? Why wasn't he more evangelistic? Why did Jesus waste a "golden opportunity?" Why didn't he make this offer at dinner in Levi's house, where he was surrounded by sinners who really needed to be free?

He didn't, though. He said it to his *followers*, and he is still saying it to us: ". . . if the Son liberates you—makes you free men—then you are really and unquestionably free." Did he say this because he thought they were "not quite saved?" Was he making the offer again, giving a second invitation to them because they had "lost their salvation?" No. He said it because he was teaching them their continuing need to discover more and more of the freedom he had already given. They were *not* free as they stood listening to him, and he knew it. They didn't know it, but he did. They were still depending upon Abraham's fatherhood for their freedom. They were still depending upon their national and religious heritage. They were following after Jesus of Nazareth, but they were not *depending* upon him for liberty. They weren't even aware of their slavery. They didn't even know they were not yet *free*. They gave him quite an argument, in fact. And he answered: "I assure you, most solemnly I tell you, Whoever commits *and* practices sin is the slave of sin."

Sin? But aren't our sins forgiven when we receive Jesus Christ? Yes. They can be forgiven no other way. No other of the world's religions offers forgiveness of sin: only Christianity. But those are past sins, and at the time of our first leap of faith we are born anew—given new life, and *all* the growing process is still up ahead. We have already said that being born is merely being put in the place to begin growth. This so obvious fact should put an end once and for all to the glib, superficial promises of "instant victory" made by some Christians in their feverish efforts to be successful pickers in the Lord's vineyard. No one can grow without birth, but birth does not guarantee growth. One highly intelligent, highly "successful" evangelist gave up his work entirely because he could not face bringing more and more babes into the kingdom only to have them starve to death in the churches. This man may be anti-organized church by now. I don't know. I am not. I am only against our refusal to make use of the freedom God offers in our own lives, even as we rush madly out to work in the vineyard.

Freedom for whom?

For us all, but for the purpose of this book, freedom for all believers *who love it enough* to take from God the liberation he holds out toward us forever. Freedom for the *unlovely* Christian, who needs, for his own sake, for his friends' sake, and for God's sake, to become lovely in Christ. Freedom for the static Christian, the feverish worker in the "harvest," scurrying from field to field, so the next "prayer letter" will sound productive. Freedom for the *superficial* Christian who praises God for the success of his business, and acts as though it is all his own doing. Freedom for the *harrassed* mother who browbeats her children into their Sunday best week after week, because "how are they ever going to learn about God and the good life if I don't get them to Sunday school?" Freedom for those stultified by conformity and fear and doubt.

Freedom for the non-believer, after he makes the turning, yes. But then, once he believes, he is in it *with us*—in the same need of growth in the life offered by our Lord Jesus Christ. We are all the "poor" whom Jesus came to set free.

HOW DO WE MAKE USE OF FREEDOM?

We make use of the freedom He offers by giving our attention to the God we know in Jesus Christ. There is more: the same God, in the person of the Holy Spirit, lives within the very being of the believer. Our bondage will remain, the prison walls will stay up, *unless* we love freedom enough to be willing to begin to let God *be himself in us.*

7 / HOW DO WE MAKE USE
OF FREEDOM?

HOW DO WE GROW in the freedom offered by Jesus Christ? How do we make use of the continuing supply of inner liberty in the wider place in which he has set us?

Surely, since no two persons are ever at the exact same point in their progress toward liberty, we need first to dare to permit ourselves to believe that God knows this. He knows exactly where we are.

They have been so numerous, I can't begin to remember the letters I have received from nervous, confused Christians —some new in the life, some old—who have come to the big crater in the road marked "doubt." They have begun to doubt that they had ever been given new life at all, simply because they did not feel "victorious," did not experience the heavenly delights of some of their more emotionally geared friends, had not received what they could readily recognize as answers to their prayers, still remained the only Christian in the family and so on and on. Most of these conscientious people say they know it isn't God's fault, that it must be their fault somehow—but how?

I have gone to the altar a half dozen times in the last two years, pleading with God to save me.

I know some are the elect of God and some are not. Please tell me how I can know that I am one of God's elect.

I am a member of an interdenominational prayer group. It is a wonderfully close-knit group, and at first I thought I had found reality in the fellowship of these devout people. But now, everyone in the group but me has been given the gift of speaking in tongues. They all feel sorry for me and assure me they are praying fervently for me to receive it too, urging me to believe that I will. The end result with me is that, now I don't know what to believe. If God has given this gift to everyone in our group but me, it can't be that he isn't willing. It must be some fault of mine.

For seven years I stayed active in my church. I did everything they told me I had to do if I was going to grow in my new life with Christ. I stopped going to movies, stopped smoking, stopped taking a social drink, stopped dating non-Christians, gave up all my old friends, read my Bible, witnessed, and prayed every day. But I have just plain grown bored with all of the don'ts. I haven't begun doing any of the old things again, but I know the reason is because I don't want the people of my church to look down on me. If I were really a Christian, I wouldn't be bored with my church, would I?

At college this year, I met a new friend who seems to love Jesus Christ more than I do, and yet she does some of the things I was always told were sinful. When we pray together, it is as though she *knew* he was right there with us. She is so close to him and I am not. Have I been wrong about myself all this time? Do you think I was really born again?

The list of questions goes on and on, the troubled person *certain* of only one thing: that he or she has in some way let God down, or "failed" in the high art of being an adequate Christian.

In the first place, there is no high art involved. There is

the human heart and God. The human mind and God. The human spirit and God. God is always in motion toward us all. It is never his way to back up, to retreat, to reject, to exclude. But he did say: ". . . *if* any man will open the door. . . ." He will not push it open. And many of us have barely cracked our doors enough for his life to squeeze in at conversion and because of a particular doctrinal emphasis, a particular church conditioning, disobedience, laziness, lack of understanding of the real potential for life in the wider place, have failed to open it wide. We have permitted our God to remain small and cramped.

Today, I received a stimulating letter from a forty-three year old woman in the western part of the United States. She had made the rounds of religious isms and fringe groups and large "accepted" denominations. For years, her mother had harangued her for being abnormally religious. Still her search went on. In each group she adapted wholeheartedly. With the liberals, she became a liberal. With the conservatives, she became a conservative. With the churches where formal ritual prevailed, she became a ritualist. In the Bible churches, she toted her Bible. She carefully followed the do's and don'ts of each group and faithfully adopted the symbolisms peculiar and meaningful to each one.

Now at last she is free.

And I, for one, am glad she tried it all out first. Hers is the healthy, open, inquiring mind which God can really light up. She is honest. She is kind. There was not one critical implication against any group in her letter—not one. She seems only to have love in her heart for them all now. The point of her letter to me was that, after reading my book, *What Is God Like?* she felt perhaps I would know what she meant when she said she believed at last she is converted to *Jesus Christ.* When, in her long pilgrimage, her new birth took place, she doesn't even care. She knows it did, because she has not stopped in her steady pursuit of freedom to love him in a way to which she can respond with honesty in her own heart. Each one of the groups who offered her their "techniques" suffered an enormous loss when she finally wandered away. When I finished reading her letter, my heart fairly sang. She will find a church where she will feel at home. This is really not her goal. She has always *given* to each of the others. She is not going to church in order that she might be pleased. She is free and wants to share her freedom. I don't think she will ever be satisfied with anything second-hand. Some might consider her a church tramp. I don't. She is simply a rather rare phenomenon in our world—an open-hearted, open-minded, intelligent human being who will settle for nothing less than the original—Christ himself. She is free and growing freer.

How do we make use of the freedom He offers? One way surely is by stopping long enough in our busy rounds of religious activity to remember Who it is who offers release from bondage. You've heard the old slogan: Man must get back to God! He must. We must slow down and become aware again of the presence of the only One who can give freedom of spirit. There is no question of God's having left our presence. I have always thought it superfluous—thought-less, for us to pray: "Oh, Lord be with us." He is always with us. "Lo, I am with you alway." A more accurate prayer would be: "Oh, Lord, help me to get quiet long enough to remember that no matter how far out I get, I am *always* in your presence."

In order to make use of the freedom we are wasting, we must simply remember Jesus Christ. I know of no better way to stop comparing your "experience" with someone else's than to remember God himself. Do you think the God who created the complex anatomy of the human body, who created stars and hyacinths and sandy beaches and snow-capped mountains and sparrows and eagles and the wind and green leaves and sunsets is going to be repetitious enough to create for you, his singularly beloved child, the same kind of experience he creates for me, his equally beloved child? Getting back to God doesn't necessarily mean having a tearful repentance scene over some lurid sin. I think we all need to return to him every day of our lives. Only he can attract us long enough to finish the work he has begun in us. We put the cart before the horse when we urge loyalty to any church. Such loyalty should come as a *result* of loyalty to the Lord whose body is the Church.

No one can be free until he or she takes time every day to become better acquainted with Jesus Christ. And there probably isn't a single Christian on earth who doesn't need this. Who can know him fully? Who can possibly understand God? Whose knowledge of him is so vast that it doesn't need to be enlarged?

My own inner freedom to act with balanced responsibility and poise in the various areas of my personal and professional life is present exactly as I am aware of the presence of God. When the mail piles up so that I begin to lug along false guilt every time I go to the mail box to pick up still more, when I have financial problems, or become impatient or critical or dull or dogmatic, I have learned that there is always just one way out of the bondage—stop everything and re-recognize Jesus Christ as the Lord of my life.

". . . where the Spirit of the Lord is, there is freedom."

Release from any kind of strain is where he is. Knowing this, why do we go on avoiding him? Acting as though he isn't there?

Release comes inevitably when we return to remembering, to concentrating on God himself. What gets our attention will always get us. And if it is true that the freedom the Son gives makes us "really and unquestionably free," why do we wait so long to give our attention to the Son?

Many people go wrong here, though, because the mere act of going back to God is not enough to free us, to teach us how to make use of the freedom he gives, unless we know something of what he is really like. This we can only know in what we learn of Jesus Christ. It is certainly true that no man has seen the Father. But it is also true that the Son has, and he has revealed him. Jesus Christ came to earth so that anyone could discover the true nature of the Father. "I and the Father are one." How could he have made it any clearer? Peter tells us to "grow in the knowledge of the Lord Jesus Christ." This is, and to me will always be, the big, shining secret. I can know what to expect of the Father if I know what to expect of the Son. I can know the Father's heart if I know the heart of the Son. If God is like Jesus Christ, then I can trust him. I didn't say if Jesus Christ is like God, then I can trust Jesus Christ. God cannot be clear to man except by *specific definition*. He is too vast, too deep, too high. Jesus came in person, to define him. To turn to a fuzzy or legalistic or vengeful concept of a being called God, can only bind us more. But ". . . if the Son therefore shall make you free, ye shall be free indeed."

We make use of the freedom he offers, then, by *giving our attention* to the God we know in Jesus Christ. There is more: the same God, in the person of the Holy Spirit, lives within the very being of the believer. Our bondage will remain, the prison walls will stay up, *unless* we love freedom enough to be willing to begin to let God *be himself in us*. We Christians are often bound by our own critical dispositions, as only one example. Turned loose on our own, even in a committee meeting where God's business is being discussed, we are quite likely to let fly with a pious-sounding, scorching blast at a fellow committee member or the minister or the minister's wife. At work, when someone steps on a Christian by overstaying a lunch hour so that his lunch hour is cut short — it is a temptation to "let the offender have it with both barrels." When the pipes freeze and the exhausted, overworked plumber is five hours late, we can forget that Christians are supposed to bear one another's burdens, as we blithely add to his by accusing him of overcharging. God, as we know him in Jesus Christ, would have his own way of handling these times of stress and strain on the nervous system: He would have a higher way available for us to use; an impossible way for us to follow without his very own Spirit acting in us—for us. God always has available the way of love: *agape* love. The love that not only identifies with the other person, but which experiences concern for him in his own particular predicament.

Permitting God to be himself in us is ruggedly hard on the human ego. We miss all the fun of "getting it off our chests," of "putting the other fellow in his place," but we find a new and freer place; a wider place in which to live at peace with God *and* the human offenders.

Making use of the freedom God offers in Jesus Christ spoils a lot of fun for our pride, dulls our skillful self-defense, hampers our loving attention to ourselves. But it results in the ever-expanding life in the wider place where peace is and where there are fewer and fewer shackles on our souls. Where we dare to live as he wants us to live—free to be our own best selves in him, not timorous, quaking imitations of each other. If we begin to make creative use of the liberty he offers, we can stop hiding our weaknesses under bad tempers and self-pity, and live as courageous children of the Father, free of doubts about whether or not he has kept his part of the bargain.

We can, after all, only know for certain that we are making correct use of our freedom, *if* the results center us more and more on God and other people, and less and less on ourselves.

DO WE LOVE FREEDOM OR CAPTIVITY?

Daniel Webster once said: "God grants liberty only to those who love it." He does. He wouldn't dare grant it to an unwilling, unbalanced, timid or rebellious spirit. And the human spirit is always unwilling, always rebellious or timid, until it knows God in Jesus Christ. A man may seem quite brave, but without a practical knowledge of what he can expect of God in his time of crisis, he will refuse to take the *free* road through it.

8 / DO WE LOVE FREEDOM
OR CAPTIVITY?

T HE SPIRIT OF THE LORD [is] upon Me, because
He has anointed Me [the Anointed One, the Messiah] to
preach the good news (the Gospel) to the poor; He has sent
Me to announce release to the captives . . . ."

But do we really care about release from captivity? In a
practical sense, are we even aware that we are captives? Has
professing belief in Jesus Christ really changed us, causing us
to dare to learn to love the freedom he offers? Do we
actually comprehend that he came from the Father to fulfil
the most important announcement ever made?

Anyone who truly loves, longs for the loved one to be
free. God loves everyone—he *is* love. If we believe this, why
aren't we more interested in the fact that *our release* from
bondage is his first concern? The potential of our freedom to
make full, creative use of the very love of God, seems to leave
too many of us bored, uninterested, unconcerned; seems to

find us too busy or too lazy or too indifferent to discover the true nature of the liberty we can all have in him.

Why is this? Is it because we are willing to settle for the easy rationalization that it is a freedom too high for us to comprehend? Is it because we have been superficially trained to think of this freedom Christ promised as being limited to some future life where everyone will sit around with nothing but "free time" on his hands? Do we limit God's interest in our lives right now on this earth by being satisfied that he has somehow set us free for eternity, but expects us to go on living now in the bondage characteristic of earth men? Have we forgotten that he came to give us abundant life—now? Or don't we care? Do we prefer our pet peeves, our right to condemn our brothers, our prejudices, our irritable dispositions to the responsibility of liberty?

Are we afraid to find out how really vast is the liberty of God?

Are we afraid to discover the nature of the liberty he has been urging upon mankind ever since the first man and woman grabbed what they *thought* was freedom and found it to be what God knew it to be all along—bondage?

When our first parents stepped out on their own, to "become as gods," they were motivated by what they saw as a desire for more freedom. "Freedom" to eat even of the tree God told them to stay away from for their own good. They were not succumbing to their love of real freedom: they succumbed to their unconscious love of bondage—the same love of bondage that still infects us. They wanted to be as wise as God, to be able to make their own decisions without him. Oh, I'm sure Adam had enjoyed his walks in the cool of the evening with the Lord God. I'm sure Eve loved the beauty around her. But they wanted what to them seemed *more.* We call it "having our cake and eating it too." Instead of remaining childlike with the Lord God, in relaxed, simple obedience, *free* to live in the perfect beauty of his love and companionship, they thought they saw a way of improving their lot. They didn't hate God, they just wanted his way and theirs too.

Does this sound familiar? Don't we enjoy the quiet, spiritual beauty of worshipping the Lord God in our expensive church edifices on Sunday mornings? Isn't it uplifting to our spirits to hear a Bach chorale sung with joy and musicianship? The sound of the magnificent instrument on which the church organist plays sends our spirits soaring. All of this is to be desired and enjoyed and it certainly is a comforting feeling that we are in God's will to go each Sunday and enjoy it.

But what about the rest of the week? What about Monday or Wednesday morning, when the organ is silent and the heavy, paneled church doors are locked? An accountant is in your office and he has discovered a few corners that can be cut on your income tax. Why not? After all, you did a lot of things for people during the last year—non-deductible things. Let Uncle Sam pay for it. He's got plenty of money. Look at all you've given him in your lifetime alone. Your accountant thinks you'll get by with it, so you feel you're "free" to do it.

Or maybe the laundry man has just come. You woke up on this bright, sunny Monday morning feeling "high and lifted up" from having heard all that glorious, elevating music yesterday at church. You hadn't once thought of your anger of last Thursday, when you opened the laundry bundle and found they had ripped two of your new percale sheets. Now the unsuspecting laundry man stands smiling at your door and with the organ silent and the church doors locked, you are "free" to give him Hail Columbia. For five minutes you stand there at the door "blessing him out good" for something over which he had absolutely no control. After all, he is the *deliveryman*. He didn't wash or iron the sheets. God in you, would have given you the *freedom* to remember this, to make your complaint like a lady, intelligently aware that all the deliveryman could possibly do would be to make your problem known at the laundry, where some action could be taken.

Are these over-simplifications? Not if we are honest about the true meaning of freedom. The Christian churchman who falsified his income tax returns—even a little bit, robbed himself of the liberty of a clear conscience. If, by any chance, his returns were picked at random for examination, as mine were a few years ago, he couldn't walk into the internal revenue agent's office with a free mind and a free conscience.

The housewife whose elegant sheets were torn had a legitimate complaint. But, as a Christian, she began her Monday shackled with the quite unnecessary "scene" at the door with the driver of the laundry truck and robbed him of his smile in the process.

Why do we dodge the *true* freedom God makes available to us for every situation, large or small? I would imagine the answer is merely that we are people—people who, regardless of our spiritual insights, our service to the church, our Bible study, have somehow missed the tremendous potential of practical freedom in God. Have missed the potential of the daily *inner* liberation which he offers. At this particular point in my own life, I don't happen to be bustling with activity in what is generally referred to as "Christian service" and, as a result, I am learning what I believe God wanted to teach me long ago: that real devotion to Christ begins first with learning to love the freedom he gives us.

Does this seem like so many words to you? Have you been conditioned to perpetual verbal witnessing? To perpetual meeting going? To feeling as though you are doing nothing for God when you are merely *being* his? Even when I was living out of a suitcase, speaking about God nine months a year, I *didn't* feel "led" to send long, mimeographed letters to my friends, ticking off "victories" and "numbers" resultant from my efforts. There were some to report, but I traveled for *him*, and felt sure he knew about it anyway. Now, if I suddenly had an impulse to write a letter for distribution to my friends and acquaintances concerning *my* activities, I'd have to write something like this: I am beginning to grow a little at last. I am learning to allow God to make some use of my increasing awareness of him. The Bible was right: His voice is a still small voice. I am beginning to listen. And what I hear has to do with *freedom*. Slowly, steadily, the bonds are dropping. I am being set free to experience reality in the wider place he has prepared for us all on this earth. I am learning to love those who disagree with me. I am learning to be more aware of the human suffering in the world, and with this new awareness is coming an awareness of God's urgency to set us free to help alleviate some of it. We cannot bless our enemies when we are choked with hatred for them. We cannot love those whose prejudices harden their faces toward us when our own faces are hardened in prejudice toward them. We cannot serve God's purpose while condemning those who, in our opinions, do not serve it. We cannot know God's love until we accept the fact of his love for all those who irritate and misuse us. We cannot be free until we stop criticizing those among us who are still bound by a fetish for doctrine, unaware of the liberating power of the love of God. We cannot be free as long as our horizons are set by the limitations of our pet opinions—political or religious. I am learning something of what Jesus meant when he declared that only "the *truth* shall set you free." These days, I find myself more "at home" with the truth, more and more willing to choose the way of love, more at home in the wider place where freedom comes as we begin to want what he wants. Where freedom grows as our love for it is permitted to draw its nourishment from the Holy Spirit of the God we follow.

Is this all I'm doing these days, you ask? Just learning to love the freedom I've been given? If I am honest, I must say that it is. Because in learning to love the inner freedom from God, one finds one's work, one's interests, one's social life, one's spiritual life, one's play life gathered into a continuing whole. In quite a different way, life becomes all of a piece. The tragedies go on occurring, the problems continue to come, people go on misunderstanding our intentions, praising us for the wrong reasons, condemning us for loving even where we can't condone; and yet, there is a melding of the bitter with the sweet, a confluence of the stormy and the quiet, an all pervasive, totally God-permeated quality to life in the freedom of the wider place that sharpens one's awareness of Who is ruling there; Who it is who unifies the loose ends; Who it is who creates the very atmosphere of freedom within us, no matter what happens outside. Paul said it: ". . . In Him all things consist—cohere. . . ." They do. The jagged times never need to cause us to forget the times of joy. The times of human happiness need not cause us to forget or neglect God. The scars and the blessings becoming one.

My life is going well at the moment. I am seeing some long cherished dreams come true. Humanly speaking, these are the happiest days of my adult life. But part of the freedom that comes from God is in learning that human happiness is not an end in itself. This is a lesson we are slow to learn. Yet as we learn it, we become free to be just as aware of the need for God in our happy times as in our times of sorrow or grief. We find it almost impossible *not* to turn to God when our need is great, but we can go for weeks when all is well, merely nodding to him on Sunday. One of the most particular characteristics of freedom in the wider place of which I write is that in it is the growing awareness of God *at all times*, with less and less effort on our part to remember him.

You see, the wider place is where the Spirit of the Lord *is*. It is not discovered without having formed the habit of looking for him first in everything.

We all suffer the disillusionment of watching more seasoned Christians seem to forget him, but no one needs to bog down in these disillusionments. Anyone who knows Jesus Christ and has formed the habit of turning to him first, can plow through the dark, question-filled times when other people "let him down." This will happen, but we do not follow other Christians, in spite of the pressures put upon us to do so at times. We follow Jesus Christ. And he cannot change or vacillate. The freedom lies in him.

Our concern is with what *we* do with the freedom God gives us, as individuals. Jesus chose to bring in his kingdom, person by person. Only in that way could it be permanent. Only until I have accepted at his hand, my own personal gift of freedom where you are concerned, can I be permanently free. Only until you have accepted at his hand, your own personal gift of freedom where I am concerned can you be free. Then I can misuse you and condemn you and hold prejudice toward you, but I will not bind you. Then you can misuse and condemn and hold prejudice toward me, but you will not bind me.

In her new, truly profound book, *Your Teen-ager and You*, my beloved friend Anna Mow writes: "For everyday living [freedom] means that I can never blame my husband or my neighbor for any reaction I ever have toward them. No matter what happens to me or what anyone does to me, my reactions are always determined by what *I am* and not by what has been done to me. My own thought and action must begin in my own area of free choice before I begin trying to reform anyone else."

We are free in the wider place, with the freedom that comes from God, when we begin to act on *what we are* in him, and not on what is done to us or against us.

We do not love God's freedom enough because we are mere *people*. And people, without the controlling Spirit of God in charge, cannot learn to love his freedom, because they cannot fully know it. We remind me of the Israelites whom the Lord tried one way and then another to set free. Periodically, they reached a state of semi-obedience to his leading, and things inevitably worked better for them. As long as the Israelites obeyed the Lord God (which they managed to do fairly well for about forty years at a time), they were relatively free to press on toward the land he had promised. The land where they could enjoy life at last as free men and women.

But there should be no parallel between our experiences and those of the Israelites. Christ *has come* to us. His Holy Spirit indwells us. The Israelites had to act on what the Spirit said to their leaders, to the prophets. Theirs was a far different relationship to God from the intimate, personal one offered now to the followers of Jesus Christ. We have direct contact with the Lord God, and look at us—still rebelling, still living superficially, still refusing the freedom to live fully as redeemed sons and daughters of the redeemer God himself. The Jews were being led *toward* the wider place, the Promised Land. The wider place is now *within* us! And still we hold back. Still we diminish God. Still we nestle down in our bonds, refusing to face the fact that we have not begun to taste the freedom God intends for us. Actually the gift of his freedom is already ours. But do we use it? Do we love freedom enough to bless people with it? Or do we keep them behind the high fences of our own opinions and pet prohibitions? Do we love the freedom of Christ enough to be willing to love our enemies? To bless those who persecute us? When we are under fire, do we love his freedom enough not to fight back? The question is not, have we managed, now and then, when someone was watching, to turn the other cheek in order to be considered "advanced spiritually?" Rather has it become a daily, *natural* habit with us? An act of love chosen freely, because of the freedom of love itself within us?

Release to the captives is available. Freedom is here, guaranteed by Christ himself; not a partial freedom now and then, but a quality of freedom that will make a man "free indeed."

Have you ever thought deeply about what Jesus might have meant when he used the phrase "free indeed?" Have you ever wondered why good people are not always generous or pleasant or kind? Could it be that they are so bound by inhibitions and prohibitions and fears that these occupy their thoughts to the exclusion of the commandment of love? God has assured us of his own strength minute by minute, so that under all circumstances we can be free to be honest, to be loving, to be patient. God provides a way for us to choose *his way* at every turn of the road. "Free indeed" means the fact of freedom in our dispositions, our spirits, our hearts, our minds. The liberty of God is a *fact*, not a trumped up, pietistic emotion or notion.

Daniel Webster once said: "God grants liberty only to those who love it." He does. He wouldn't dare grant it to an unwilling, unbalanced, timid or rebellious human spirit. And the human spirit is always unwilling, always rebellious or timid, until it *knows* God in Jesus Christ. A man may seem quite brave, but without a practical knowledge of what he can expect of God in his time of crisis, he will refuse to take the *free* road through it. He will refuse to be free, even in his suffering, as God was free to stretch himself on his cross.

To love liberty means to welcome the responsibility it brings, to welcome the God-control it requires, to welcome the discipline that results from it, to welcome the maturity it creates. To love liberty enough to make use of it, a man must learn to accept being misunderstood, to accept criticism with grace, to take the blows and abuse that come inevitably to everyone in the same Spirit in which Christ took the blows at the place called Golgotha. To love liberty, a man must bless and never permit himself the luxury of cursing—not even in pious tracts that defame and smear the characters of the elected officials of his government or church.

To love freedom, a man must love Christ enough to permit God's Spirit to live his human life on earth, as God would live it. To love freedom enough for God to dare to grant it a man must be willing to permit God *to be Himself* in every act of his human life.

A man cannot learn to love freedom this much overnight, but he can learn a day at a time, and a day is as a thousand years to God.

TO SEE AGAIN

Only by checking our spiritual eyesight can God continue to give new light. He gives it according to how much he knows we are willing to take and absorb and use. If you have suddenly realized that it has been a long, long time since you have experienced some new light from the Father, you can be sure it isn't his fault. Be honest — how long has it been since you have given him your full attention? How long since you have looked only at Jesus, the author and finisher of your faith?

9 / TO SEE AGAIN

JESUS SAID THE SPIRIT of the Lord was upon him to "announce release to the captives, and recovery of sight to the blind."

What did he mean?

Surely, he meant that he would heal men and women whose physical eyes were blind to the world around them. Simply by flipping through the pages of the gospels, one can find repeated instances when Jesus gave back sight to those who were blind. He could not be undisturbed by physical blindness. After all, he created the sky and the sea and the green of the land. It is he who set in motion the chemicals and the moisture and the heat and the cool that cause the beauty of a sunset . . . that cause a sunset to be different every evening, no two the same. It is he who flung the stars in place in the blue-black night. It is he who hung the full moon to shine on the water whose boundaries he set. It is he who created the faces of our loved ones . . . all to delight our eyes, to give meaning to our physical seeing. More than that, it is

97

he who gave us perception to see beyond the mere physical forms around us, beyond the actual faces we love into the hearts behind them; beyond the beauty of nature into his heart. It is he who thought up the shining gift of human imagination, to heighten our sight of mere clouds accumulated in an evening sky: to cause us to "see" ships on a bright green sea and islands and lines of trees in the wind-torn strips of cloud. God is all for the creative use of our imaginations. We glorify God when we see "more than meets the eye" in a sunset or a sunrise. We glorify God when some long-curbed impulse to create floods our very being as we stand on the side of a snow-covered mountain and feel the poetry of the straight, tall pines coursing through our very souls. Most persons who long to write perhaps shouldn't try. Most persons who long to paint, have no real ability, add little to the realm of art. And yet, it delights God's heart for us to "see" beyond and beneath what merely meets the human eye: to form into words, to transfer to a canvas or a song these longings to enter into his creation in our small ways is not a bad thing. It is a good thing. It is of God and it glorifies God. The point is not that it must be read or seen or heard, this stirring within, when we behold the beauty of the Lord around us. The point is that the stirring *occurs*, and that it occurs in human beings whom the Lord has made. Perhaps one of God's great sorrows is that our first parents preferred their own way more than they preferred to stay in the midst of the beauty with which he surrounded them.

God enjoys our physical seeing; he enjoys our response to what he has set before us. Jesus opened the eyes of the blind when he was on earth so that they could see again. Why there are blind people still on earth, I do not know, but I have long ago stopped the superficial questioning of physical handicaps. It is superficial, I am convinced. Although I do not for one minute believe God sends physical blindness to anyone, I have seen that, because his ways are higher than ours, we can only safely begin our *explanations* at the point where he began to demonstrate redemption: at the cross of Jesus Christ. If we begin with creation, nothing comes out right. No one's heart rests. But if we begin our attempts to cope with human tragedy at the place of *redemption*, the unfolding goes on and on. Our "whys" are caught up in his great why as he hung on the cross. They are not only caught up in his own why shouted to the Father that bright-dark day, they are diminished, ultimately silenced by it. My questionings are lessening every day of my life. It is not that I know the answers, it is just that I am being caught up with him into the wider place where I am being freed of my questions. In the wider place with him, the angry "whys" slip into praise and thanksgiving. In time we realize it is no longer necessary for us to question. It is not that we change our question to "why not?" We merely realize that the "whys" do not come any more, because *God is there in it all.*

God is there in every person's sight returned by surgery. Neither the patient nor the surgeon needs to be a Christian for the Christian God to have been in the healing. Perhaps Jesus is healing in different ways now, but he is healing: by science, by surgery and, of course, by prayer. That he is a healing God I know with all my heart. I merely believe that we somehow free him to heal if we do not attempt to confine his methods to any one way.

God *cannot* be confined, but our efforts to box him in can block his access to us.

Jesus' interest in physical sight goes on, but we are here concerned with the healing of the eyes of our spirits. In every act of his when he was on earth, in every word he spoke, in his every attitude, Jesus Christ preached the healing of the human spirit. The restoration of sight to those who are blind to God's truths, to God's ways. He is still the same Lord. In the person of his Holy Spirit, God still walks the earth announcing release to the captives of spiritual and mental darkness; announcing recovery of sight to the blind.

Have you noticed that Jesus phrased his announcement as though we had all seen once at some time in our existence and then had lost our spiritual sight? I'm not sure that this is a pivotal point, but surely it is a provocative one. And when God can provoke us to thought about him, he has accomplished step one in the restoration of inner sight. (Conscious, energetic thought about God is evidence that we are *in* the wider place with him.) Jesus did not say that he came from God to announce that men would see for the first time. He did not express it that way. There is no implication that man has been spiritually blind from the beginning. Rather, the announcement clearly states that Jesus was anointed by the Father, to *restore* sight: ". . . to announce release to the captives, and *recovery* of sight to the blind." A captive, to be a captive at all, had to be free at one time. For a man to see *again*, to have his sight recovered, he had to have gotten back what he formerly possessed. After all, man *was* once in harmony with the Lord God. If God is the source of our human existence, then in the beginning we were whole *in him*. He is, in us all, then, about the recreative business of restoring us to what he intended us to be in the beginning.

Somewhere, sometime known only to God, we did *see*. We were able to understand by the light of heaven itself. *We* brought on the darkness, but this did not stop him. He remains at work, giving light, restoring our ability to see.

Those among us who came into this light and found our spiritual sight restored after we were adults, can tell you about how foolish we felt at times with all the new seeing. I think "foolish" is the right word here. At least it is the correct word to describe how we felt when, in the first days after we opened our beings to the light of Jesus Christ, we *saw* as fact, as truth, as reality, the things we had always hoped were true, were real. We saw them so clearly, we felt foolish not to have seen them before! Felt foolish, that is, until our sight cleared still more and we came to see that only as the veil is lifted from the inner eyes of every man, does he see. Still, there was this strange familiarity: as though sometime, somewhere in our existence, we had caught at least a glimpse of what we now saw with such clarity. It is not even a tribal remembering, an accumulative memory handed down through our heritage; it is sharper than that, more focused. It is of God. And although it isn't a true remembering, it is "familiar" from that *sometime*, that *somewhere* when we were still a part of the mind of God himself. New Christians are not at all surprised that Jesus Christ called himself Alpha and Omega, the beginning and the end. They know it is true.

That first sight after conversion to Christ is clear where the basics are concerned: our own sinfulness, our own helplessness, our own desperate need of a Savior. And instead of making us shudder and cringe, this first sight gives us rest. Anyone who has truly had his sight restored by Jesus Christ soon stops despairing over how sinful he was, soon stops thinking "What if Christ hadn't been there to save me?" He stops these useless thoughts, not out of spiritual pride or ingratitude, but out of the growing wonder that Christ was not only there to make the initial rescue, he is still there, giving more and more sight. He is *still there*, being the light by which we can continue seeing more and more. He was there in the beginning; he will always be there: he is the beginning and the end.

Why, then, are so many of us *lacking* in spiritual sight? Why do we squint when God's light is upon us, upon some truth he is eager to make plain? Why do we insist upon using the spiritual bifocals of visiting speakers and spiritual counselors, when God wants us to learn to see for ourselves? Now, obviously, I am not inferring that we should not listen attentively to the messengers of God, that we should not seek counsel, that we should not read books. We should. But we tend to depend too much and too long upon this second-hand seeing.

Anyone who has for one reason or another been put into the usually uncomfortable place of spiritual counselor can understand what I mean when I say that many such persons have discovered the hard way that they must be willing to be misunderstood. There comes a time when offered friendship, even offered counsel becomes a weakening instead of a strengthening experience to the person who needs help—a blinding thing. The Israelites clamored for Moses to speak to them, lest they hear the voice of God—anything to avoid a personal confrontation with the Lord God. Christians are still doing this. We buy books and attend meetings and make counseling appointments right and left—anything to keep us from having to undergo firsthand, the clarifying, cleansing experience of new light from God. Our spiritual eyes are too weak to take his light. And we have weakened them by the overuse of *spiritual eyeglasses*.

We have developed a neurotic dependence on the minister, the Sunday school teacher, our favorite authors. It's much easier to let them dig out the insights and then pass them along to us. God wants to give sight to us firsthand. This is the only way we can really possess it. Now, I certainly don't mean that whatever you have seen from the reading of this or any book, is necessarily not from God to you. Books and sermons are among his many ways of speaking to us. But we do need to learn to exercise the eyes of our own spirits more. Only by checking our spiritual eyesight can God continue to give new light. He gives it according to how much he knows we are willing to take and absorb and use. If you have suddenly realized that it has been a long, long time since you have experienced some new light from the Father, you can be sure it isn't his fault. Be honest—how long has it been since you have given him your full attention? How long since you have looked only at Jesus, the author and finisher of your faith?

Now, this is not to suggest that God is going to give us some kingdom-shaking new truth every day. If he did, he would only make more work for himself, because we would become so spiritually vain about our perception, our ability to see "the hidden things of God," he'd have to begin work on our pride. What we are attempting to pin down is how long has it been since you have, right in the midst of some daily duty or on the way to the grocery store in the family car, focused on God to see if he has anything new to add to the errand you're on right then? Realizing God in the mundane is, to me, one of the most distinguishing characteristics of the authentic Christian. It requires nothing whatever of us but turning our attention to him for a split second. The inevitably creative, redemptive results are certainly nothing to our credit. The results are simply what a person who really knows God, learns to expect.

Let me give you the most recent example from my own life —as recent as today. I worked late into the night last night on some correspondence and other work that needed to be done so that this morning I could give complete attention to this chapter on *seeing*. Just as I was ready to enjoy breakfast, Elsie Goodwillie, my good neighbor and secretary, knocked on our door with a message from the gentleman who is supervising the hauling of fill dirt and the grading of the land where I am building my home. "John Golden wants you to come right up to the property. There are some decisions to be made this morning." I hurried through breakfast with the tension mounting inside. Normally, any excuse to leave my desk and drive the ten miles up beautiful Frederica Road to the house site is fine with me. Today it was a different matter. But I hopped in my car and headed (too fast) up the road, my mounting irritation over my upset plans to write first thing this morning showing up "plain as day" in my driving.

I had gone about three miles when I began to smile alone in the car. What was being accomplished by my resisting the trip? It had to be made. How ridiculous can one get? Now, there is nothing that turns my mind to God more quickly than feeling ridiculous, so I began to focus directly on him. I *didn't* ask him to slow me down or give me this chapter more quickly than normal to make up for the lost time. I didn't surrender a single thing. I just turned my attention to him and of course, he was there. And suddenly, I was *seeing* the morning sunlight slanting through the branches of the giant live oak trees on each side of the road, lighting the thick, gray moss waving in the day's new breeze from the ocean. The light on the island has become a familiar symbol to me. It is the nearest thing to his light in my heart and mind that I have ever seen. It shines for *now*, beautifying the woods and turning ordinary marsh grass and weeds into jewels, but it also has a ray of eternity in it for me. And here I was, scooting up my beloved Frederica Road, exceeding the speed limit, *missing the light*. Missing the light on the trees, so like the light within—until, I took one simple step. Automatically my foot eased up on the accelerator. Wasn't I writing a chapter on *seeing?* And doesn't there have to be light before one can see? I laughed. I think God did too. After a most pleasant few minutes with Mr. Golden, and two more errands intended for later in the day, I enjoyed the *light* all the way home, and am enjoying it still right now, as I write these words to you.

Do I consider this an important insight from God?

Yes. More important than if he had given me an entirely new idea for another book! This I need every day in order to live adequately. This kind of seeing *you* need every day in order to live adequately.

Our part in spiritual seeing involves one thing and one thing only: we are to give Jesus Christ our attention in the midst of whatever is happening. Turning our attention toward him is not always as easy as it was for me driving along in the beauty of the morning light on St. Simons Island. I have learned, though, that even in the midst of a tirade of criticism, or an argument, it is still possible, *if* we truly believe in the redemptive nature of the God we follow. His mind is on Viet Nam today, on all the over-burdened government officials of all the countries of the free world; it is on the enemy too. His is the kind of mind that can concentrate fully on everything at once. His mind was on me in my small, relatively unimportant frustration. It is on you in yours, small or great. And *if* we turn, we will find that his announcement was right: he has brought recovery of sight to our once blinded eyes.

Spiritual eyes that have been restored to Jesus Christ can "see in the dark." If you are one of those in the thick darkness of a religious conditioning which has blinded you to the signs of God in those who do not see exactly the way you have been taught to see the things of God, he can, *if* you are willing to give him your attention, restore even your clarity. Everyone who becomes a believer in Jesus Christ is just not going to abide by all your group's prohibitions, by all your doctrinal emphases. But God will not permit himself to be limited. You can limit your own vision of him; still he stands by right now, to restore your sight, to lift the scales of uneasiness from your inner eyes, to relieve you of the tension of fearing to be disagreed with.

God will do this if you are in the darkness of political or racial prejudice, of grief, of heartbreak, of business pressure, of failure. Our part is simply to look at him. He is always there, always available, always ready to keep his promise to restore our sight. To set us free to see again.

OUT FROM UNDER

It is a great stimulation and encouragement to me that God did not stop with promising merely to *deliver* from oppression and tragedy. He went further, as he always does, to make his promise totally creative: he *sends forth* those whom he delivers, giving their lives purpose, new meaning, needed responsibility.

10 / OUT FROM UNDER

JESUS DID NOT COME from the Father only to preach the Gospel to the poor and to bring back sight to the blind; he came to "send forth delivered those who are oppressed—who are downtrodden, bruised, crushed and broken down by calamity."

He came to "send forth delivered" everyone who struggles under a burden too heavy for him to carry. God came in Jesus Christ to bring us out from under whatever weights us down, whatever keeps us inadequate, whatever downgrades our spirits.

The load you carry may be a consequence of your own doing. It may be the direct result of someone else's sin. It may be merely that you are a victim of the haphazard—a phenomenon which certainly exists in our universe, whether we are flexible enough to admit it or not. You may be under a cloud formed, perhaps, inside your own mind. Many, many otherwise cheerful, creative Christians find their lives shadowed by this kind of mentally depressive cloud. It can

109

only be hoped that you see clearly enough on the days the cloud lifts, to realize that this is no cause for guilt feelings on your part. The very fact that the Lord Jesus promised to leave his joy with us, does not mean you are failing him when your own outward joy ebbs under the shadow the inner cloud throws over your spirit. Any of us who are fortunate enough never to have experienced this kind of depression can be thankful. But if you do experience it, take heart! It need not last. God has help for you in a competent and qualified doctor. I firmly believe this kind of practical help is from God. All positive help is from God. "Every good gift . . . cometh down from the Father of lights, with whom there is no . . . shadow of turning." God has said he will bring us *out from under* whatever *oppresses* us and this has to mean also that he will, by whatever means he has at hand, bring us out from under whatever *depresses* us. If it is a state of mind requiring medical help, by all means get it. We should all go just as freely to psychiatrists and psychologists as we go to internists. There is no shame involved. If we feel there is, then we are still influenced by the dark ages where mental disturbance was considered a mark of disgrace. God has set us free of this old wives' tale in our modern society, and I wonder if we don't insult his gift of freedom when we feel false guilt at obtaining the proper care for our mental disorders.

In Part III of this book, we will be looking in some detail at God's ways of bringing us out from under some of the common reasons for a burdened heart. Christians can and should gain all the ground possible by an intelligent pursuit of facts. We should use our God-given intellect to think through the reasons why we are not adequate to our daily round, to discover our true motivations, to accept help at the hands of a professional, if necessary, so that we may come to the place of understanding our failures, our insecurities, our rebellions, our hostilities. But it is at this point that psychiatry and psychology stop and God must take over. A good therapist can bring out our hidden twists and show them to us, but only God can *redeem* what is found to be the source of our problems.

Only God is a redeemer, and only God believes in the re-demptive process enough to have given his life on the cross to prove it to us!

Have you ever thought about God's own faith in redemption?

Only recently have I begun to think about it and the wider place grows still wider as I continue to dwell on it. Neither in this chapter nor in the chapters in Part III where we will be more specific, dare we stop with the discovery of our real problems. Not even with the clear sight of them, not even with recognition of them, not even with our determined efforts to do something about them. We dare not stop any-where short of the redeemer God himself. If we do, the mere sight of our quirks and foibles and rigid eccentricities can harden our personalities against ever coming *out from under* the burden of our weighted lives. Certain inflexible patterns, still unbroken from old conditioning, will set more firmly and we will flee still deeper into the prison of our humanity, dodging the freedom God offers.

"I cannot bring myself to go to church anymore," one man said. "I'm afraid to. All my life God has been preached as a God of vengeance who will make me pay for my own sin. I know this is not what he's like, but because I want to know so much that he loves me, I'm afraid to stick my head in a church for fear I might hear some of the old stuff again."

And so we run back still deeper into a darker cell in the prison of our conditioning.

"I refuse to have my doctrine shaken by just any old wind. I refuse to get my feet tangled in any new ideas about God. You may call me self-righteous, but I just stay away from those groups who yack, yack, yack about a God of love. I guess I know he's a God of love without their telling me."

Exaggerated? No. Underplayed. And both of these peo-ple are destroying their family life. One by nurturing fears, the other by nurturing self-righteousness. Both sense their real problems—fear and self-righteousness; both are under tremendous burdens in their relationships; both are refusing to go honestly to God for liberation.

Jesus Christ announced boldly that he came to deliver those who are oppressed. He did not say that he came to deliver *some* who were oppressed. Jesus never limited his offer to a few. "For God so loved the (whole) world, that he gave his only begotten Son. . . ." God is too big to be exclusive. Because his mind is every minute in intense concentration on each human being in the world, he can never offer deliverance to a select few.

This seems to be the place in our thinking for us to settle once and for all, the fact of God himself. If he is a God of love, as the Bible declares, then he is always in motion toward everyone in existence. Love is always in motion toward us, to deliver us. To set us free—if not from the outward cause of our burdens, to set us free in our inner selves so we can cope with pressures from the outside. God is once and for all involved with you. God is once and for all involved with me. God is once and for all involved with everyone we know; with everyone we don't know. He is involved with our loved ones and he is involved with those we despise.

More than that, God is committed to us forever and ever and ever.

How much have you thought on that?

I, for one, have heard so many sermons and have read so many books which hammered away at the necessity for *me* to commit myself, that I almost don't absorb them any more.

Does this shock you?

It won't if you stop to remember God. If you will stop to recognize the danger that all this emphasis on *our part* can, if we are not very, very careful, minimize God's part in his life with us.

Last summer at the Christian Booksellers' convention, I was asked by Bonnie Hanson, a dear friend of mine who edits *Floodtide* magazine, to write an article for her on the need for a totally committed life in the believer. I smiled, knowing that her brand of Christianity was not the inflexible variety, and said: "No, I can't do that. I've done it, and it only came out making me sound as though I had somehow managed this kind of total commitment. I find I'm no longer laboring over my commitment to him. What has my attention is God's commitment to us!"

Her eyes brightened. She will use part of this chapter in her magazine. She saw it and because I believe her to be an authentic Christian, her seeing confirmed mine.

Before we go further, let me assure you that I still believe in the necessity for us to commit ourselves as fully as we know how to Jesus Christ. He told us we were to take up our crosses and follow him. Our commitment to him is not in question here. If we are to be delivered from oppressions, from the tragedies that confuse and batter us, from the calamities that bruise and break us, we must first be convinced —not of *our* commitment to him, but of his eternal *commitment to us*.

If we are not convinced that God is once and for all totally committed to us, his children, we cannot only fall unwittingly into the "Oh, I can't bother God about my small problems" habit, we can also draw back in doubt of his touch because our pain seems too terrible to trust even to God.

Here again, my one favorite theme—the key to all the mysteries of all of human life as I see it: the *necessity* of learning what God is really like.

If, in Jesus Christ, we have come to see the depths upon unfathomable depths of the love of God, aren't we more able to trust that love? If, in Jesus Christ, we have seen God himself identifying with all human suffering on the cross, with all human temptation in the wilderness, with all human misunderstanding as he stood tricked and betrayed before his own—if, in Jesus Christ we have seen even something of the lengths to which God has gone to quiet our fears of him, to choke off our doubts, to persuade us to come freely—can't we then come more freely with our oppressions? Our bruises?

Our calamities? Our griefs? Our heartaches? Our failures? Our shame?

"I can't bring my grief over my husband's death to God because I can't be sure he understands it."

Does that sound presumptuous to you? To me it sounds honest. How can we be sure God understands the pain in our hearts if we don't know him personally? How can we know he will understand merely because we have heard someone say from a pulpit that he does?

As I see it, there is only one answer to any question about God: look at Jesus Christ.

The woman who couldn't bring her grief over her husband's death to God because she couldn't be sure of his understanding had no real reason to be sure of it! She simply did not know Jesus Christ and God are one and the same. When she came to see that they *are* one, rather than adding false guilt to her already over-burdened heart, she brightened up. One small ray of hope had entered her crushed spirit. She had never heard it put that way before. God existed, she didn't argue that point. She argued nothing, in fact. She was too shattered for argument. Nothing could bring her loved one back. He was gone from her sight, from her arms. She would never hear his voice again. Never sit at breakfast with him, never read aloud to him. Their life on earth was ended—suddenly, and he was gone forever from her presence. She was not bitter. She was crushed with grief. She smiled wanly when God's name came up. It was as though her intelligent, gentle mind turned to the idea of God's comfort for a brief moment, then discarded it. Not in anger, not in rebellion, just discarded it as one more sedative that wouldn't work to lessen the pain of her grief. God? No, she couldn't turn to him, simply because she *couldn't* be sure he would understand her pain.

I understood her discarding the idea of turning to God, understood it fully. There was no way she could be as sure as she had to be that God *would* understand. I knew he would, but she didn't. This was no spiritual achievement on my part at all. I simply had discovered a few years before she did that anyone can know this God who promised to bring us *out from under* our calamities. She knew it too, within a few days, and God's progress with her was swift. She brought no barriers with her, no lop-sided religious conditioning—she just brought her intelligent mind, her needy spirit and her broken heart. He was there, of course, to deliver her and he did. Not by the magic action of a waved wand over her shattered life, but by daily increasing her faith as God daily convinced her more deeply of *his commitment* to her in her sorrow.

He did not bring her out from under one burden only to cast her under another, either. A young man I know came to believe in Jesus Christ as God after losing his wife and child in an automobile accident. God helped him through his time of weeping, made him want to live again, but when some of the edge wore off his sorrow, he began to question God about the accident. "I almost wish I hadn't come to believe in God at all," he wrote. "If I'd just gone on believing there was no God, I would have just said it was an accident and let it go. Now I know there is a God, and sometimes I wish I could fight him because he won't tell me why he took my family away from me!"

This man's dilemma wasn't difficult to understand either. He had begun to believe in Christ, but unfortunately had joined a church where orthodoxy reigned instead of Christ. Where legalism ruled instead of love. Where misguided people assured him again and again that he must stop grieving because, after all, God had taken his family away from him and wasn't God always right?

People who did not think, or who thought superficially cast this young man under his second intolerable burden. God did not cause his grief. Accidents happen! The woman who met God at her husband's death was more fortunate. Her new life was nurtured among Christians who let Christ's commitment to them strengthen their commitment to him. They were *thinking* Christians who remained teachable, who did not thrive and grow fat on their own pat answers based on rigid concepts of the Father; who "worshipped him in spirit and in truth," trusting him for more truth and more lessons from his Holy Spirit among them. God was boxed into no pet doctrine of their own. The only point of truth on which they insisted is the only point of truth around which Christ builds his kingdom: the fact of his deity. They were Christians convinced that anyone could discover the true nature of God the Father through living in daily, open-minded contact with God, the Son. So far as I was able to learn, this woman never once thought to ask God *why* her husband died of a heart attack. She was too involved in discovering *how* the redeemer God was going to go right on making creative, redemptive *use* of her grief. She was too involved with Jesus Christ to question God.

She was out from under her grief, her hopelessness, her burden. She still misses her husband daily; this has not changed. But she is absorbed, not with death, with new life. New life with a God she knows to be totally committed to her. A God she can know, a God she can readily trust.

Not long ago, she smiled and asked: "Do you remember when I said I couldn't turn to God because I couldn't be sure he would understand?"

This old uncertainty was almost too dim to her now to recall. It seemed far away, remote, belonging, as it did, to another life.

He brought her *out from under* her lack of understanding, her uncertainty; he used her grief to do it. I could not say that God took her husband in order to do this. I do know that she is *out from under* her once darkened understanding and living again in the wider place with the God whose commitment to her she never questions.

"The Spirit of the Lord [is] upon Me, because He has anointed Me . . . to send forth delivered those who are oppressed—who are downtrodden, bruised, crushed and broken down by calamity. . . ."

". . . *to send forth delivered* . . . ." Set free to begin to live.

It is a great stimulation and encouragement to me that God did not stop with promising merely to *deliver* from oppression and tragedy. He went further, as he always does, to make his promise totally creative: he *sends forth* those whom he delivers, giving their lives purpose, new meaning, needed responsibility.

If God only brought us *out from under* our troubles and left us there, we could fall beneath a new oppression, or wander aimlessly toward nothing. Our God is a redeemer God, who makes creative use of even our oppressions and then, with new courage and a new heart, he sends us forth— to live again, convinced of his total commitment to us.

MORE THAN A SERMON

Jesus came to bring us the message of the Father toward us all: "to preach the good news. . . ." But he did more than preach the greatest sermon ever preached, he came himself to *be* the good news of heaven to earth.

11 / MORE THAN A SERMON

JESUS STOOD IN THE SYNAGOGUE in his home town of Nazareth to read from the Isaiah scroll:

"The Spirit of the Lord [is] upon Me, because He has anointed Me [the Anointed One, the Messiah] to preach the good news (the Gospel) to the poor; He has sent Me to announce release to the captives, and recovery of sight to the blind; to send forth delivered those who are . . . downtrodden, bruised, crushed and broken down by calamity."

Jesus stood before his old friends and neighbors to read the familiar words—to make the divine announcement. He preached the sermon of God himself that day, but he did more: he stood before the small congregation (as indeed, he still stands before the world) *being* the message of God to all mankind, *being* the Good News, *being* release to the captives, *being* the recovery of sight, *being* deliverance to the downtrodden and the burdened.

The sermon we hear today that changes our lives, that sets our goals, that does more than give us a warm emotional

121

feeling which fades before the noon meal is over on Sunday, is the sermon that confronts us with God himself. The book that gives us practical insight into how to live adequately, creatively, is the book that holds up God himself, as he is in Jesus Christ.

Doctrinal explanations of "how the Lord works," "how man is saved," "how to surrender to the will of God," etc., are all valid in their places and before the right groups, but the one message for everyone—Christian and non-Christian alike, is the message that God *is* in Jesus Christ. That Christ's coming is deliverance to the captive, freedom for all those who will assume the responsibilities freedom brings.

The chief danger in centering too much on doctrines about Christ is that we become proudly rigid in evaluating ourselves and our ability to comprehend them. Some Christians seem almost to worship the doctrines of the church. We become like the object of our worship. If the God we worship is wholly definable within the framework of our doctrines, we can become inflexible, deaf to all new ideas, blind to the relentlessness of love in pursuit of the loved one as Christ is in pursuit of the human heart. "I always turn down invitations to speak before that group," a minister once said to me. "There isn't a man or woman in it with sound doctrine." I wondered to myself (knowing that if I expressed myself to him I would crash against his wall of rigidity), why it was that if he felt himself so "right" about God, he didn't jump at the chance to share God with the people he felt were so wrong. Rigidity had so set his heart it could not open except to ideas that matched his own. He worshipped his own "correct doctrine" and it showed even in the tense lines around his mouth.

The message of God to all mankind is not centered in a doctrinal explanation; it is centered in the Son, and the Son goes wherever there is need—particularly where he is not agreed with. One cursory reading of the gospel accounts verifies this. The religious people, the i-dotters and the t-crossers,

called Jesus a glutton and a wine-bibber, but he went anyway to the irreligious as well as to the religious.

Many Christians worship the *power* of God. It is true
that if we miss recognition of his power, we miss him. And
yet, God does not follow our human concept of power in his
conduct toward his loved ones. God never barges in, push-
ing aside all who stand in his way—all who would keep him
from having his way. He stands at the door and knocks; he
stretches out his hands "all the day long toward a rebellious
people," crying: "Behold me, behold me!" Even on the
cross, he did not call down the power that could have rescued
him. He controls the infinite power of the universe, power
too vast for us to perceive, and yet his greatest show of
strength is in his almighty meekness. His is the strength of
the sure knowledge of truth. He knows he is right. Nothing
shakes him. Jesus Christ has no need to fear being proven
wrong, no need to defend himself. He could stand before
Pilate in the power of utter silence, and wait for Pilate to condemn himself. He could kneel before his disciples in the
Upper Room on the night before he was crucified, and lose
none of his power, none of his authority by washing the
horny, calloused, dusty feet of the men he loved, and Judas
was included in that love. God's kind of power is not
measured by force, not proven in manipulation, not manifest
in violence. The religious person who shoves his way
through, verbally or by his actions—manipulating his co-
workers, confusing God's will with his own bull-headedness,
has never experienced the true power of God in his own life.
If he had, he could not go on smashing hearts around him,
digging in his heels at every disagreement with his pet theories. The power of God can wait, can woo, can heal, can
make tender; can give strength to endure, strength to bless
and not curse. The power of God grants perfect freedom.
We are free to disobey him, to flaunt our egos, to give pain
to our friends. God grants this kind of freedom too. And,
we on our own, *will* disobey God, because on our own we
are not powerful enough to obey a God who commands that

we *love*. We find it much easier to dominate than to love.

If we worship *only out of our own concept* of the power of God, we have missed the message of God in Jesus Christ.

What about our concept of God's *goodness?*

"God has really blessed us this year in our business! Our profits are up fifty percent over last year. We really do praise the Lord for his goodness to us!"

Sound familiar?

Pathetically so.

I hear it in one form or another at least once a week. Christian businessmen even make public speeches on the theme. And for the most part, I believe them to be sincere, but utterly superficial in their concept of God's *goodness*. Now, I am not suggesting that we should not thank God when our bank accounts bulge and our profits soar. We should thank God for everything. But what about God's goodness to the Christian whose business fails? Or whose profit is only ten percent or twenty percent? What about the Christian whose job of fifteen years is jerked out from under him by the religious institution for which he works? This happens, you know, and what about God's goodness there? Doesn't God love the failures, the downtrodden, the semi-successful, the mistreated among us as much as he loves these who can count their financial successes in large figures?

Where do we delineate? If I write a book that sells extremely well, am I not to praise God for it? Yes. But I am not to worship the results of God's activity, I am to worship God. I am not to misconstrue the success of a book for God's *approval* of me! I have written books which have sold well and I have written others which have not sold so well. Am I to praise God for the ones whose royalties have disappointed me when pay day comes at the publishing house? *Yes.* Because we are told in the *New* Testament to thank God for everything—good and bad. And this pricks the thin balloons of praise sent up by the glib brothers who praise God for their increased business success, implying that somehow they are "living right" and God is rewarding them. To me, it is far more profound to admit to a measure of ability on our part, to recognize that certain economic laws are in operation in our world and we have simply come up with a good product or a popular service or a well-written book that sells. This does not diminish God. It glorifies him because he is much more interested in making us honest than he is in "making us money!"

Others among us seem to worship God's *protection*. We live long lives, with a minimum of illness and trouble and forget the cross in the New Testament entirely. Instead we become "Old Testament centered," and decide that we must be living "pretty good Christian lives" because God has protected us. "Well, there's only one answer," a Bible teacher once said to a woman in deep sorrow over the lingering death of her husband. "Your husband didn't live right before his conversion. We can't expect God's protection unless we live right. Our sins will find us out." If this weren't so cruel, it would be laughable. Did Christ "take" Mary Magdalene's earthly life because of her sins? Did he cut Peter off from the land of the living because he denied his Lord? No, he set them both free to begin giving his love to everyone. Who *does* "live right" before conversion?

We all know people who blithely declare that God prevented their deaths or the deaths of their loved ones in automobile or plane accidents. It is true that all good things come from the Father, but again, what about those Christians whose lives were lost in the same or similar accidents? God works in the haphazard. He reckons with accidents, with coincidence, with human carelessness and human neglect. Accidental death to anyone could not be called the perfect will of God, but he does not change the laws of physics just because Christians are involved. If a Christian gets too near the edge of a high cliff, he will fall over. God's laws are consistent. Both his physical laws and his spiritual laws.

God does protect his own, but not always in the ways we expect or recognize as protection. Peter Marshall was a young man when he died, and Jim Elliot and Dr. Paul Carlson and

Peter and Paul and Lincoln and John Kennedy were murdered. The worship of God's protective powers as a kind of
super insurance policy can become one of our major distortions of the true message of heaven. We cannot explain
these things, we can only be willing to think deeply and
calmly and rationally enough to realize we cannot force God
into even our clearest concepts of him.

There is only one explanation of God and that is in *Jesus
Christ*, the Messiah, the Anointed One.

There is only one explanation of deliverance from the
oppression and that is also in Jesus Christ.

Others among us worship God's *love* and this comes the
nearest to being a valid worship. "God *is* love." He does
not merely have a loving heart and nature, he *is* love.

John, the beloved disciple, writes of the love of God as
though he could not bear to stop writing about it: "Beloved
let us love one another; for love [springs] from God, and
he who loves [his fellow men] is begotten (born) of God
and is coming (progressively) to know *and* understand
God—to perceive and recognize and get a better and clearer
knowledge of Him. He who does not love has not become
acquainted with God—does not and never did know Him;
for God is love."

*"He who does not love has not become acquainted with
God. . . ."*

I remember a sincere, hard-working Christian brother who
criticized my admiration of another Christian brother, equally
sincere and hard-working: "Stay away from those *love*-birds!
Love isn't the way to recognize a true Christian. The only
way to know a man is a real Christian is to watch the number
of souls he wins!"

And this brother who let go the tirade on love was one
of those who "worshipped" the Bible so much that he seldom
walked across the room without tucking it under his arm. I
cannot say he merely carried it and didn't read it. I know he
did read his Bible. But neither can I say how he managed
to read it as much as he did, to revere it as he did, and still

have missed finding out what John had to say about love. He did not write: "He who does not win souls has not become acquainted with God." John, who had laid his head on the very heart of Christ during their years together on earth, wrote: "He who does not *love* has not become acquainted with God."

And yet, although God *is* love, and although I believe love is lacking in much of Christendom, there is a danger here too. Some persons, who refuse to face their need of a Savior from sin, concoct their own idea of God's love and make it central, thereby turning God into a beneficent, indulgent Grandfather who says, "there, there" to everything we do. Nothing could be further from the truth about God's love. In his love is embedded his holiness, his hatred of anything that harms his loved ones, and for God to condone destructive behavior in us would be impossible. Loving us with the kind of pure love only he possesses, the kind of pure love only he understands, he must also show us the strict side of his face, or we would destroy ourselves.

I read some literature recently from a particular group "founded on love" as the masthead claimed, and in the literature was the story of a man who found the woman "he truly loved" ten years after he had married his wife. This man, a leader in the group, had rationalized God's love to the extent that he now felt "led of God" to divorce his wife and desert his three children because "God is love."

Even God's love—his central characteristic, can be distorted beyond recognition if we worship our idea of love alone.

There are also groups who seem to worship God's *holiness*. These can become as extreme as the others. In their sincere and intense pursuit of what they recognize as "holiness" they endeavor to become as different from the rest of us in behavior and appearance as possible. I remember when one of my earlier books came out with a picture of me on the back of the dust jacket in which I happened to be wearing small earrings, the publisher received a letter from a "holiness" group saying they had sold hundreds of copies of the book, but they did hope that in the next picture, I would not wear earrings because they had to sell the books without the otherwise attractive dust jacket! To them, with earrings I did not have the "appearance of holiness." The saving grace of these dear people is that they go on loving me and accepting my love, but God's holiness does not make us peculiarly different—it makes us whole. It gives us the natural grace to live our days in the moderation and balance and good taste which only his Holy Spirit can impart to the human mind.

We dare not worship merely his holiness or we will miss the whole of God's message to us.

In fact, worshipping either the protection, the power, the holiness, or the love of God separately or alone—is unrealistic. There is simply no way to know the nature of the true power, the true protection, the true holiness, the true love of God outside of Jesus Christ. Much *more than a sermon* is involved here: the message of God *is* Jesus Christ himself.

"No man has ever seen God at any time; the only unique Son, the only-begotten God, Who is in the bosom [that is, in the intimate presence] of the Father, He has declared Him —He has revealed Him, brought Him out where He can be seen; He has interpreted Him and He has made Him known."

Jesus Christ and Jesus Christ alone has revealed the Father. In his person is the "fullness of the Godhead bodily." In his person is the goodness of God, the intention of God, the heart of God, the power of God, the holiness of God, the very attitude of God toward all creation.

Jesus came to bring us the message of the Father toward us all: "to preach the good news. . . ." But he did more than preach the greatest sermon ever preached, he came himself to *be* the good news of heaven to earth.

PART III

To proclaim the accepted *and* acceptable year of the Lord
— the day when salvation and the free favors of God
profusely abound.

Luke 4 : 19 (The Amplified Bible)

FREED FROM CONFORMITY AND RIGIDITY

Thoughtless, automatic conformity to one's own religious circle can be just as deadly as conformity to the world. Not outwardly, perhaps. But inwardly, and the rigidity from the stultifying patterns set by one's religious conditioning, however "sound," can prolong the deadly influence for a whole lifetime.

12 / FREED FROM CONFORMITY AND RIGIDITY

IN THIS LATTER HALF of the twentieth century, the word *conformist* has almost become an insult. If one is a conformist, one is considered imitative, unoriginal, dull, without individuality.

Perhaps we should consult the dictionary before we go further: to conform means, "To make or be like; to bring into, or be or act in harmony or agreement." The synonyms for the verb *conform* are: adapt, agree.

Is it bad to act in harmony or agreement? Is this an undesirable trait? That, of course, depends upon the nature of our conformity. Paul said we were *not* to be conformed to this world, that we were to be transformed by the renewing of our minds.

"Do not be conformed to this world—this age, fashioned after and adapted to its external, superficial customs. But be transformed (changed) by the [entire] renewal of your mind —by its new ideals and its new attitude—so that you may prove [for yourselves] what is the good and acceptable and perfect will of God, *even* the thing which is good and acceptable and perfect [in His sight for you]."

I have noticed that Paul took no chances whatever on our being able to learn how to *conform* successfully, without rigidity, to the right things or to the "right people." He knew only *transformation* was safe. And this is the point I hope to make here concerning the only possible way to freedom from the rigidity which inevitably results from plain old *conformity*.

Paul did not say we were to be *conformed* even to Christ. True, conformity does imply agreement and adaptation, but if we are honest, I doubt that any man on earth can say he completely agrees with or is adapted to Jesus Christ. Especially not where he, the man, himself is concerned. It's possible to agree with Christ's commands for other people, but only the consciously or unconsciously dishonest Christian will say he is in total agreement, total adaptation, right down the line. If he were, he would obey Christ totally, right down the line. Do you? Do I? Does anyone you know obey completely?

Could anyone *conform* to Christ unless his mind had been *transformed by* Christ?

Not just "sort of" transformed, but "changed by the entire renewal of your mind." Jesus Christ, when left to do his highest in a human life, never settles for half-way measures. He is not about the redemptive business of renewing your mind to make you Baptist or Methodist or Roman Catholic or Lutheran or Presbyterian. He is about the business of renewing your mind so that "you may prove [for yourselves] what is the good and acceptable and perfect will of God, even the thing which is good and acceptable and perfect [in His sight for you]."

Does this sound as though God is interested in erasing our human personalities, our intellects, our individualities? Does this sound as though he wants us to conform to each other or to our pet "fellowships?" Does this sound as though he wants

us all "to do this" and "not to do that?" As though he expects
all Christians to pray alike? To be baptized by the same
method? To understand the Scriptures in exactly the same
way? To dress alike, act alike, talk alike, think alike?

". . . so that you may prove [for yourselves] what is the
good and acceptable and perfect will of God . . . [in His
sight for you]."

Obviously, this does not imply that we are to go winging
off in a dozen directions, acting as we please, thinking as we
please, interpreting the Scriptures the way we prefer them to
be. Paul did not say we were to become rebel *nonconform-
ists.* He urged "the entire renewal of your mind." Such a
complete renewal that it amounts to a transformation, a
change. Such a complete renewal that by its *new* ideals and
its *new* attitudes (the very ideals and attitudes of Christ) we
can then prove for ourselves the good and acceptable and
perfect will of God for each one of us.

Once we have caught some of the depths of this truth, it
no longer remains difficult to know the will of God. I
rather imagine one of the most frequently asked questions
among Christians is: "How can I be sure this or that is the will
of God?"

In case you care to take the Apostle Paul's word for it, he
says we can know *only* by the renewal of our minds. Only
by the transformation of our ideals and attitudes. Paul says
we are not to be conformists; we are to be transformed. Now,
we cannot transform ourselves; we can only conform. So
here again, we can stop our feverish self-effort and give
God a chance to be himself. He *can* transform. Only he
can. If we began with all diligence and earnestness to change
our ideas, our ideals, our attitudes, one at a time, we would
not have enough time to finish the job in eternity. That is, *if*
it were possible in the first place. We can have our minds
changed, but it is always, if we are honest, due to some outward influence. Our political thinking can be changed (unless we are hopelessly conformed to great-grandfather's
views), but it is changed by exterior circumstances, by the

views of the men running for office, by the new party platform, by social conditions in our country, our state, our cities.
We don't normally sit down and change our minds for no
reason. An outside influence is always involved, but the only
outside power which can completely change the mainsprings
of our minds and hearts is Jesus Christ himself.

Conformity, then, is the easy way. It requires less of us.
We simply look around for a group or custom with which
we agree, or with which we feel comfortable, and begin
conforming. And it must be remembered here that we are
not discussing conformity as against nonconformity. A non-
conformist is in reality, a conformist to nonconformity. I
know. I have, in the past, prided myself on my nonconformity. I now see that some maturity of mind would put an
abrupt end to the beards and fantastic hair styles of the young
men and women who flaunt what they believe to be their
nonconformity. They are in reality conforming one hundred
percent to each other. Just as parents are conforming, who
insist upon their young people conforming to the "nice"
behavior of the church young people, or making the "accepted" social contacts. It is an insult to the God who created
no two palmprints alike for anyone to attempt to influence
anyone else to *thoughtless* conformity.

"Naw, she's not one of us," a young lady in an office
sneered. "She sits all through her lunch hour and reads her
Bible! Can you imagine?"

What's wrong with reading one's Bible on one's lunch
hour? There is no better literature available anywhere. The
Bible is the world's all time best-seller. If this girl were
to read Shakespeare, she would no doubt be shunned as being
peculiar too. But what is really wrong with reading one's
Bible in public? Why does it always seem to make other
people uncomfortable?

Now, before you begin to condemn the girls who laugh
at the Bible reader, consider this remark made by another
young lady in a midwestern high school: "Oh, she *says* she's
one of our group, but the rest of us carry our Bibles every-

where we go—right on top of the stack with our other books. She *never* carries hers. She even eats lunch with that smart-aleck gang who always make fun of our fellowship meetings."

What's wrong with *not* carrying a Bible everywhere one goes? What's wrong with eating lunch with the young people who need to find out that a Christian can be a normal human being too? What's wrong with *not* appearing "special" and "righteous?"

Thoughtless, automatic conformity to one's own religious circle can be just as deadly as conformity to the world. Not outwardly, perhaps. But inwardly, and the rigidity from the stultifying patterns set by one's religious conditioning, however "sound," can prolong the deadly influence for a whole lifetime.

"Do not be conformed to this world—this age, fashioned after and adapted to its external, superficial customs."

Few will argue the fact of the superficiality of the world around us. But Christians desperately need to see that there is just as much conformity to superficiality in religious circles as in the world. Paul is telling us here not to conform to *anything external* or *superficial*. The kingdom of God is within us, or Jesus was wrong. It is our attitudes, our ideals, our inner motivations that need *transforming* before we can know the perfect will of God. Before we can be free. Before we can learn how to live safely in the wider place with God. And in all honesty, we have to admit that the external, superficial attitudes and ideals of the world have invaded our churches, our religious publishing houses, our religious institutions, our religious thinking. I doubt if it is really a recent invasion. Let's face it, it has been there a long, long time.

Christians will hire a cleaning woman for a miserably low wage because "this is the going wage around here" and suffer no compunction of conscience whatever: conforming to the external attitudes and ideals of the community. Christians in lucrative businesses impress upon their employees in pious tones, that: "We know we don't pay quite as much as some places, but after all, you are working directly for God in our establishment and he will reward you in heaven." In too many areas, Christians practice the same lack of ethics as the world.

Conformity to this world is always deadening. It is deadening to the human conscience, deadening to love, deadening to freedom, deadening to human relationships.

We can't honestly blame non-Christians for conforming. We do, but we can't if we stop to think. They do not have access yet to the *transforming power of Christ.* "Oh, no, *they* don't swear or tell their dirty jokes in front of me," a Christian man boasted archly. And he was boasting too! Does this sound like the God who stretched his arms out to the whole sinful world on the cross?

There is nothing realistic about a Christian acting superior under any circumstances, but most particularly, is he dodging reality when he threatens non-believers so that in his presence they stop conforming to the ways of the world. And the Christian, who demands conformity to himself *is worldly.* No one can stop being conformed to the world *until* he has been *transformed* by the entire renewal of his mind. And this is only possible through some intelligent thought and the deep, continuing working of the Holy Spirit of God.

He, and he alone, can free us from conformity and the inevitable rigidity that accompanies it. If you know a man is a dyed-in-the-wool Republican or Democrat, religious Liberal or Conservative, don't you attempt, when possible, to keep the conversation away from either politics or religion? Who walks blithely into a conversation about the Federal Government with a member of the John Birch Society? Or who deliberately brings up the Civil Rights issue with a member of the White Citizens' Council or a militant SNCC disciple? No one, who doesn't want to be battered by a rigidity that yields to no reason, no intelligent exchange of ideas, no exchange at all—just a one-sided tirade from a mind closed and locked by conformity to his group or his ideas or his attitudes of heart. God doesn't attempt to change a man's politics or his denominational preference. This is not transformation. God is about the delicate, long-suffering task of changing our inner attitudes of *heart*. He wants to give us the attitude that says: "Well, I certainly don't agree with you, but you're entitled to your own ideas on this. Why don't you share them with me?"

One of the sure signs of conformity is the locked, rigid mind. One of the sure signs of transformation is the open, humble, teachable mind.

If we are even in the process (and sometimes it is a long one) of allowing the sensitive, strong, reasonable Holy Spirit of God to transform our ideals and inner attitudes, we are entering the wider place. The wider place where the Spirit of the Son is striving to make us free indeed.

FREED FROM MERE OPINION

There is a vast difference between the merely opinionated and those with strong convictions based on the truth God offers in Jesus Christ. And the difference is demonstrated most often in love or lack of love. If we are living in the safe, free, wider place with God, we cannot be swayed from what we have seen of truth, but neither can we go through our days with our fists doubled, ready to strike out at anyone who challenges our opinions.

13 / FREED FROM MERE OPINION

HOW MUCH OF WHAT YOU believe about God belongs to you as *truth?*

More subtly, how much of your faith is regulated by mere opinion? Do you obey God because you love him and believe his purposes will ultimately be vindicated? Or do you obey him because everyone else in your circle "obeys" him in certain *opinionated* areas?

Our tendency to conform slides easily into the area of our opinions. We settle for the *opinions* of other people rather than the freedom of knowing the truth. But Jesus said: ". . . you will know the truth and the truth will set you free."

When we act on what we *know* of *truth*, we often create discomfort around us, but *if* we are acting on it in the Spirit of Christ, even in the midst of the discomfort, we generate hope. Just as the sinner is made restless, agitated, under the relentless love pursuit of God, so is he—at the same time—made to feel that if his whole world crashes, there will be kindness there, a holy welcome for his heart.

If we are acting on opinion only, we cause discomfort and it is cold discomfort; repellent, unattractive, binding, to us and to other people.

The friend who led me to Christ remained loyal to him in every area of her thought, her confidence; but she also remained *kind* with me, even hopeful. I believe she was able to do this only because she was acting on truth and not merely her own opinion.

Only God's opinion could be based wholly on truth.

We are simply not flawless, either in our minds, our hearts, or our attitudes. The tireless worker in the "harvest field" who spends himself compulsively to win other people to Christ, can get his ego so involved in whether he wins them or not, he becomes *opinionated* instead of remaining motivated solely by truth. He is bound and not free. He binds and does not free.

Only "the truth will set you free."

In the preceding chapter on the freedom from conformity, when we mentioned the radical men and women who plunge either to the right or the left politically, toward any extreme religious viewpoint, we were speaking also of the *merely opinionated*. It is humanly impossible to dislodge them from their rigid convictions that *they are right*, totally right, and anyone who disagrees with them on one little point is totally wrong. In *their opinion* everyone else is immediately suspect. Suspect of what? Oh, whatever happens to be the target of their opinion. They leave no room at all for the middle ground. No room at all for those who believe only God has all the truth and only God is completely correct in his judgments. They permit no learning on the way. They tolerate no open minds. If a mind is open, they are dead certain the wrong facts will slip in. Their God is minuscule. He cannot possibly influence his children in the right direction *without them and their opinions* which are worshipped as truth.

"Don't talk to me about having an open mind," a retired gentleman once wrote from California. "Just as sure as you leave your mind open, a germ will get in!' "

I am of the belief that God can enter an open mind too. And I'll place my faith in him and not in the "germs."

"That fellow is just as sweet as a man can be, but I don't think much of his salvation." This from an evangelical "leader." When I asked why, he said: "He doesn't believe in eternal security. He thinks he can lose his salvation!" Arguing on neither side, because I was then a new Christian and hadn't heard about these contradictory opinions concerning God, I grinned and commented: "But *you* believe he's secure, don't you?"

Opinions.

Opinions are not secure. They are always influenced by our environment, our friends, our teachers, our special corners in which we sit mulling them over. Opinions bind. They do not make free. We are prone to make free with our opinions, but they do not make us free.

"I simply don't trust that man. I don't like his face."

I once loved my English bulldog more than anyone I knew, and anyone—no matter who it was—just anyone who didn't like English bulldogs, I mistrusted.

"We're not renting to *them*. They're white, but they're members of the NAACP."

"We only hire 'born-again' Christians here. He would have been a good man for us too, as far as his ability, but he goes to that liberal church, when he goes anywhere."

"You can always tell a man by the company he keeps. I put my foot right down on my daughter's dating him. He claims to be a Christian but when my husband and I had dinner out the other night, there he was at a table with some other men and *they* were drinking beer!" She wasn't sure her daughter's boy friend was also drinking beer, but "you can always tell a man by the company he keeps."

They called Jesus a glutton and a wine-bibber for the same reason.

"We don't care for our new preacher. He just takes one text at the beginning of his sermon and never reads another passage from the Bible. Our former minister quoted Scripture steadily."

"I never heard such laughing and singing as comes from the house next door since those new people moved in. We're just sure they're drinking."

"We wouldn't consider publishing a book by him. It would sell, but he isn't 'sound.' At least he wasn't the last time I heard."

We jump like rabbits to conclusions, form opinions around them, never bother to find out the truth and away we go: binding ourselves, binding those around us so they are afraid to express their own thinking. Our friends are afraid of an exchange of ideas with us because we are afraid.

Some men of science rule out religion. The one-sidedly religious rule out science. God is in both. The balanced end is blend. But when we have been conditioned from childhood to hold a certain set of opinions regarding behavior—what's ladylike or gentlemanly and what isn't—when we have been conditioned from childhood to hold a certain set of opinions about politics, religion, science, education, God can attempt to shake us out of it, but unless we *want* to be free, we will not be.

"I will never change my opinion about this Civil Rights issue because I like things the way they have always been," a woman wrote.

Well, this is honest anyway. But have you noticed that when we encounter someone with rigid opinions, and *the* touchy subject comes up (whatever it may be), it is as though someone had suddenly screamed? No one has, literally, but I always feel that tingling sensation as though there has somewhere been a scream. Smiles vanish from faces, lines appear, tensions twang. It is like *fear*. Is it not possible that the extremist in any area of life may carry a deadly *fear* that just because his opinions are being challenged, he might someday be faced with the discovery that something could have been wrong in his thinking all this time?

Humility enters here. The genuine humility God gives

frees us, opens our minds for an intelligent exchange of ideas. The person with the genuine humility of God does not always have to be proven right. God-given humility can say quickly: "Oh, I was wrong about that, wasn't I?" Humility can laugh at itself. It does not take itself seriously all of the time. Humilty isn't conscious of itself at all.

Opinionated people are never humble. They can't be. The humility of God neutralizes the rigid self-righteousness of the merely opinionated.

Overly opinionated men and women cannot walk in the wider place with God. It isn't that they aren't welcome, they are. Everyone is. But it is free there, and they are slaves to the bondage of their opinions.

We should think specifically every day on the *difference* between mere opinion and truth. It is only the truth that makes us free. It has been said that God does not need fighters, he needs lovers. Men and women who love truth will stand firm in their convictions, but there will be no sharp edges in their attitudes to repel those who are still in darkness.

There is a vast difference between the merely opinionated and those with strong convictions based on the truth God offers in Jesus Christ. And the difference is demonstrated most often in love or lack of love. If we are living in the safe, free, wider place with God, we cannot be swayed from what we have seen of truth, but neither can we go through our days with our fists doubled, ready to strike out at anyone who challenges our opinions.

God does need lovers, not fighters, because he needs strong disciples and there is eternal strength only in love.

FREED TO BE NATURAL

We hear it said that "you can't teach an old dog new tricks." Perhaps not an old *dog*. But we are *human beings,* made in God's image. Men and women who, regardless of our self-inflicted prisons of immaturity, can be released by the power of God if we want to be released. Can be set free by the supernatural so that we can become *natural,* elastic, adaptable, easy-to-live-with children of the Father.

14 / FREED TO BE NATURAL

HAS IT EVER OCCURRED TO YOU that the average conformist among us and the average sharply *opinionated* person are both apt to be childish? Not childlike, childish. *Unnaturally* childish. Paul wrote to the Corinthians at the close of his singular passage on the character of love: "When I was a child, I talked like a child, I thought like a child, I reasoned like a child; now that I have become a man, I am done with childish ways and have put them aside."

Do children imitate each other? Isn't one of the starkest heartbreaks to a little girl *not* to get a new outfit for a special occasion when her friends all get one? If he can't go ice skating because his mother thinks it's too cold, doesn't the small boy's world crash because all the other boys' mothers let them go? It is desperately important to children to conform. It is *natural* for them to conform. They are just discovering themselves and it helps them cope with new findings if their friends are participating in the same discoveries. They are just discovering that new clothes make

151

them look attractive, that in order to capture and hold a place of popularity and recognition, they must be *on hand* when the skating party takes place. This is utterly *natural* for the very young. They reason entirely from the point of view of themselves: of what *they want*, of what they think is desirable. Not what mother knows to be best, but what they want at the moment. They have not yet learned to consider the thinking of other people. Their reasoning is *naturally* all one-sided. Their opinions are strong and noisy and they fight to protect them; fight to protect them because these newly forming opinions are their very identities in the process of daring to become known—recognized.

"When I was a child, I talked like a child, I thought like a child, I reasoned like a child. . . ."

Is it any wonder, then, if to cling stubbornly to mere opinion just because it is ours, to conform to the herd simply because we want its safety and recognition, are strong characteristics of childhood, that those of us who continue it into our advancing years are troublesome and ridiculous? These traits which are so natural to the small child are equally unnatural to the adult. Such traits are difficult enough to cope with in children; they are almost impossible in adults.

"Now that I have become a man, I am done with childish ways and have put them aside."

Maturity. Maturity of mind and emotion to match the maturity of our years. Maturity of mind and emotion to cause us to be *natural* at the very center of our beings. The difficult, hard to handle grown man (or woman) is inevitably *immature*. He causes unnatural tensions around him because he, a man of thirty-five or forty-five or sixty-five, is acting like a small boy. He is reasoning from his own point of view and solely his own. He is demanding that life fall in line with *him*. He causes the rest of us to step carefully around his personality because he has *not* put away childish things.

Jesus said: "Truly, I say to you, unless you repent (change, turn about) and become like little children (trusting, lowly, loving, forgiving) you can never enter the kingdom of heaven at all."

Is this a contradiction? No. It is the other side of what Paul said about the necessity of ridding ourselves of *childish ways*. The *childlike* nature of a child is his real one, the nature given by God to cultivate and nurture into maturity. The *childish* nature of a child is the false one he acquires in his struggle for recognition. Christians with the very Spirit of God within them, should have no problem discriminating here. When we dare to think it through, it is embarrassingly clear. We are to remain *childlike* in our humility, our ability to trust and to forgive, but we are to lay aside the *childish* traits which are no longer *natural* to us as adults, and which prevent our friends and families from being able to be *natural* when we're around.

Other than the need to conform and the need to cling to mere opinion, what are some of the other signs in so-called adults that keep them from being natural?

Surely one of the most cantankerous of *childish* traits in men and women is the tendency to *dramatize* things all out of proportion to reality. The tendency to "make a big deal" out of an ordinary event. To pout for hours over nothing. Do you dread hearing a certain familiar voice on the other end of your telephone wire simply because you know he (or she) is going to take half an hour (or more) to tell you in exaggerated self-pitying detail of something that happened to him? With some people, a headache with all the resulting complications is good for at least twenty minutes narration. A bad cold can cause others to build enough material for a three-act play. "My husband has a recurring backache as a result of an accident years ago and am I being unsympathetic when I sometimes lose patience with him and ask him just to let one day go by without reminding me that his back hurts?" Wives tell me husbands get sicker than other people, even with minor ailments. But I've certainly known some women who enjoy their miseries and who can fill pages in letters and waste hours on the telephone dramatizing them. These immature adults do not stop with physical ailments either. If the childish trait is clinging, it goes to work on how unpleasant their neighbors are, how many dogs desecrate their flower beds, how careless are other drivers, and so on and on and on.

We all have our share of frustrations, illnesses, disappointments, irritating neighbors, but some of us never get a chance to tell about them, and perhaps it's just as well.

To dramatize a situation is natural for children. It is unnatural for adults.

To *sentimentalize* is also natural for children and equally unnatural for adults. And yet many of us indulge in what eventually becomes shallow sentimentalizing. A grief, a sorrow, a failure can be worthy of great sentiment at first, can leave its mark forever in our memories, but if we persist in nurturing it through sentimentality, after awhile it becomes obnoxious to our friends and families, harmful to us. Bereaved persons prolong their bereavement this way. Perhaps they believe they are honoring their dead, but the man or woman who makes regular and frequent trips to a cemetery, who continues to celebrate old memories on anniversaries and birthdays, is indulging in childish masochism. Children enjoy burying their pets, adorning the little graves, preaching funerals, weeping together. They are learning about sorrow and this is natural for them. To weep is natural for adults, but to nurture our weeping, to continue seeking sympathy by sentimentalizing our grief is not only harmful to the person who is indulging in it, it creates an unbearably *unnatural* situation for our friends and families.

"I've invited my new neighbor to have coffee with us," a hostess once told me. And for almost two hours, the neighbor forced us to spend detailed time at the bedside of her dying husband, took us step by heart-breaking step through his funeral. We "went with her" to the cemetery with fresh flowers once a week for his grave; we even learned the particular dinner she still orders in their favorite restaurant where she goes every anniversary of their wedding. It was sad, and I was sorry that she was alone, but after she left, I just had to ask my hostess *when* the man died. "About ten years ago I think," she said. I had one more question. "Does this women know about you?" My hostess smiled. "Not much. She only moved into the neighborhood last month and I haven't had the chance to tell her yet."

The friend in whose home I was staying had lost not only her husband, but her two children in a boating accident the summer before. Her grief and shock had been intense, but she was not nurturing them. In all honesty, she was trying to take the release God offered her in the passing of time, in the search for a new life. The neighbor made us both uncomfortable in her childish *unnaturalness*, her sentimentality. My friend, who had three times the reason to mourn, encouraged and cheered me every minute we were together.

Our tendency to sentimentalize keeps us from recovering from our heartbreaks, our disappointments, our griefs. And it certainly keeps our friends aware of our *unnaturalness*.

Dramatizing and sentimentality are only a part of what keeps so many adults in the awkward, immature childish state. Perhaps the basis for both is our tendency toward general *unreality*. This is a particularly incongruous trait in a follower of Jesus Christ who came to set us free from the unreal, the false, the imagined, to give us the courage and elasticity to face things as they are. And yet, for example, we all know many Christians who seem genuinely surprised when they encounter dishonesty. It is as though they go glibly through their daily rounds expecting nothing but honesty in their fellow man; expecting virtue from everyone, taking personal offense if they don't find it. I can think offhand of three ministers who will launch at the slightest opportunity into a dissertation on the acts of dishonesty they meet at the hardware store, the local hospitals, in the ads from the mail order houses. They take personal offense, as though the sly tricks they have observed were directed at them only. They fume and retell the stories and once more, the familiar *unnatural* situation is set up, the familiar tensions are generated for everyone within hearing distance.

If men were *naturally* honest and virtuous, would Christ have had to die? Why should we be surprised to find dishonesty? chicanery? Why should we be shocked unless, for any of a number of real or imagined reasons, we are going around in a state of *unreality?*

Christians not only tend foolishly to expect total honesty and virtue when there is no *realistic* reason to expect them, they also tend (and perhaps none of us is immune here) to expect too much of themselves. Now, I am not suggesting that we become careless or lower our standards. We are making another point entirely: the person who expects near perfection of himself, will always let himself down. Then, he is forced into a speedy rationalization to cover his weakness. In order to get his mind quickly back onto personal virtue, he may become overly generous, may force himself to make a round of sick calls or something else which strikes him as noble—anything to reinforce his deflated ego.

Children who displease their parents will hurry to do some unusually nice thing for mother or father—to make amends. This is *natural* with children, who have not yet learned how to face life or themselves realistically. It is *childish* and *unnatural* for the adult.

There is no prison in which the grown man and woman can live which is more stifling than the prison of *childish immaturity*. We hear it said that "you can't teach an old dog new tricks." Perhaps not an old *dog*. But we are *human beings*, made in God's image: men and women who, regardless of our self-inflicted prisons of immaturity, can be released by the power of God if we want to be released. Can be set free by the supernatural so that we can become *natural*, elastic, adaptable, easy-to-live-with children of the Father.

FREED FROM INDECISION

No one always makes the right decisions. We all make wrong ones, unwise ones, careless ones. But our God is a redeemer God. If we have made a decision sanely and rationally, as nearly in his will as we know, *even if it turns out to have been all wrong,* he will not waste our mistake! He will make use of it somehow. God will teach us from it, he will temper us in its consequences, he will give us the wisdom to make another more nearly correct decision the next time.

15 / FREED FROM INDECISION

MEN AND WOMEN who have difficulty making choices are often intelligent and otherwise adequate persons. Unlike the highly opinionated brother or sister who batters one with his or her pet theory (never dreaming it could be wrong), the *indecisive* person often knows his need. And so, although the bondage is just as great, there may be more immediate hope for the indecisive than for the opinionated.

Undoubtedly, being indecisive is a childish trait, and I have seen persons helped merely by facing this fact; by carefully making note of the other areas of their lives where God has been permitted to give maturity and then by beginning to expect him to do the same where their abilities to decide are in question.

If you are indecisive, if you seem to make one choice only to replace it with another, don't push the panic button. It may require a blast of some sort to shake loose the opinionated man or woman, but a blast is just what you don't need. You need quiet, calm reasoning with yourself. If indecisive-

159

ness is the inevitable result of a rather wholly immature emotional nature, don't increase your fright by working away at this one weakness. If it is only one of a few areas of immaturity, *seeing* that it is, should start you on the way toward freedom.

Inability to choose is an unmistakable hangover of childish *dependence*. It is so much easier to have someone else make the choice for you. But even though indecision is a childish trait in the sense of clinging to protective dependence, it is childish in another way too. Children, quite unconsciously for the most part, will go to almost any lengths to get attention. Dare to ask yourself if this is why (however unconsciously) you tend to run wildly from one friend to another in a frantic effort to get them to make decisions for you. This could be the reason you don't have many friends. We are to bear one another's burdens as Christians, true. And yet, each one of us is responsible for his own decisions. While your more mature friends try to listen and to help, those who make decisions for you are only contributing to that childish state of dependence. Don't tempt them that way! It's always easier to tell an indecisive person what to do than to guide him into the art of learning to use his own "decider."

If you are indecisive, you are perhaps unconsciously wanting attention, you are certainly childishly dependent, but have you ever thought about a still simpler explanation? Simpler and sometimes just jarring enough to the human ego to set one free of it: the chances are you run to friends for your decisions simply out of "plain old habit." It worked once and you tried it again and now you are hooked.

Do you want to stay hooked?

Do you want to go on imposing on friends, taking their time, expecting them to drop everything and make the decisions only you can make? Certainly only you can *keep* your decisions once they are made. But think about it. Maybe you *do* want to go on in the same old routine.

I've moved too far away now, but for years, a certain few people in Chicago would deposit themselves regularly on my doorstep expecting me to make up their minds for them. In one of my earlier books is the story of the young lady who called the night before her wedding was to take place—the announcements were out, the rehearsal over, the church decorated, but still she called: "Do you really think I should go through with this marriage?"

I believe she has grown up since then. Her marriage is a happy one, but if it had turned out unhappily, I am inclined to think my friend's answer was the right one: "Yes, go through with it! Even if it's a mistake, just once go straight through with something you've decided upon!"

There is a particular kind of freedom in being able to make a decision and stick with it, minus the "what ifs." What if it doesn't work? What if it only doubles my problem? What if the dress doesn't please him? What if my mother doesn't agree? What if I find I can't afford it? What if I get sick? We all have a life of "what ifs" to cope with. You are not alone. *No one* always makes the right decisions. We all make wrong ones, unwise ones, careless ones. But our God is a redeemer God. If we have made a decision sanely and rationally, as nearly in his will as we know, *even if it turns out to have been all wrong,* he will not waste our mistake! He will make use of it somehow. God will teach us from it, he will temper us in its consequences, he will give us the wisdom to make another more nearly correct decision the next time.

Fear, perhaps, motivates much of our indecision. But fear in the Christian is an insult to the God of perfect love because "perfect love casts out fear." In a later chapter we will discuss the freedom God holds out for all of us who are bound by *fear.* But our emphasis at this point is on the fact that *indecision* comes from carelessness about one's own maturity.

And if we are careless about our own maturity, we are care-less about God himself. God wants us *free.* Does it begin to be clear that the freedom in the wider place of which we speak is *synonymous with maturity?* It is, and the sooner we learn this, the more progress we make toward life in the wider place where the freedom God longs to give is forever opening out around us.

One of the sure ways of developing maturity in ourselves is to throw off the *limitations* that still cling from childhood. If we have been spoiled in our childhood, permitted to have our own way, we tend, as adults, to make snap judgments. To decide too quickly, to decide and act on impulse. We want a thing, so we decide to go after it, expecting someone else to pick up the pieces if things go wrong. For this type of person, a touch of indecisiveness would be a blessing. But there is a more subtle danger if, in childhood, you were hemmed in by an overdose of parental discipline. Perhaps you were a minister's son or daughter and your entire mode of conduct *had* to be restricted by "what the people would think if the minister's child did this or that." You were robbed, in the very years when you should have had the liberty to learn to make your own choices, of *any freedom* to be your real self. What happens later? One of two things, according to a friend whose childhood was pinched by the limitations so frequently a part of life in a pastor's home: either you continue to be fearful of making your own decisions, or when you do, you immediately feel guilty for having made them. You are on your own, free at last from "what the congregation will think," but saddled with a new bondage—guilt. Now, it seems that this can happen *simultaneously* with what appears to be an opposite reaction: you are free from that artificial childhood bind, and now you are so determined to be free, to make your own decisions your own way that you become bullheaded!

It should be no surprise to discover these two contradictory patterns at work. We are not simple. We are complex and the sooner we realize it, the sooner we will begin not to expect simple answers to our problems. The sooner we realize our own complexity the sooner we will realize that to find the liberation God has for us, we must *use our minds*. Accepting our complexities should also send us running to God.

Because only God can sort out our contradictions and make us whole.

The tendency toward indecision is not always a sign of weakness. It is not always our need for attention. But it is, I believe, always some form of *immaturity*, some shackling hangover from the curbs and restraints of our childhood. It is seldom, if ever, in the normal mind, a downright *inability* to decide. As my friend, Anna Mow, says: "We all have *choosers* and they have to have exercise if we aren't going to remain childish." And sometimes we only need to believe we can use them.

If you are fighting indecision in your life, ask yourself one question: *Am I a follower of Jesus Christ?*

Are you?

Can you answer Yes to that question? If you can, isn't it just possible that you only *think* you don't know how to make decisions? Haven't you already made the most difficult decision man is ever called on to make?

"If any one desires to be My disciple, let him . . . take up his cross and follow Me."

You will never have to make a bigger, more life-changing decision as long as you live. If you have decided to follow Christ, you can make the other decisions required of you.

Could it be that you are still in the prison of indecision not realizing the power already at your disposal to decide? Could it be that you have gone blithely along being indecisive from habit, *not* reckoning with the very power that was there to enable you to decide to follow Jesus Christ? God is interested in *every* decision you have to make.

Could it be that you have just never thought this through? If you find that this is true, don't waste time in despair. Just begin now to permit God to give you brand new freedom in the area of your choice. This would be a good time to begin: by *deciding* right now, once and for all, to live forever in the wider place, where everyone is free to *choose* God's way, and where *everyone* has access to God's power to make decisions.

FREED TO WELCOME RESPONSIBILITY

Responsible Christians are balanced. They neither overdo nor underdo. In fact, although we must place our willingness to act behind our love, truly responsible persons have long ago learned that before the *doing* must come the *being*.

16 / FREED TO WELCOME RESPONSIBILITY

ALL PEOPLE WHO REFUSE to take responsibility are not merely lazy or shiftless. Most of us who carry streaks of irresponsibility are simply in bondage to our own lack of knowledge of ourselves and the freedom God offers in the *love-motivated* life.

Jesus said quite clearly that we are to *love*: "I give you a new commandment, that you should love one another; just as I have loved you, so you too should love one another."

He not only commanded us to love, he declared that the quality of our love will be man's singular guide to the quality of our Christianity: "By this shall all [men] know that you are My disciples, if you love one another—if you keep on showing love among yourselves." "This is what I command you that you love one another." "I have loved you [just] as the Father has loved Me; abide in My love—continue in His love with Me."

Jesus was preparing his disciples for his departure, and his theme was love.

You and I may clutch tightly the doctrines of our faith, we may receive and share heavenly insights, we may sharpen and keep stimulated the brains God gave us, we may live in hope of eternal bliss, but if we do not love, we will not be recognized as disciples of Jesus Christ!

Paul saw it: "If I [can] speak in the tongues of men and [even] of angels, but have not love [that reasoning, intentional, spiritual devotion such as is inspired by God's love for and in us], I am only a noisy gong *or* a clanging cymbal."

We have all known what the world calls "great Christian leaders," men and women famed for their ability to expound the Scriptures and set forth the doctrines of their faith. We have known some of these leaders who had love and their love blessed us more than their knowledge. We have known others who have lacked love. No matter how a man trains his mind, studies his Bible, exerts his leadership, if he is not minute by minute drawing on the very love of God shed abroad in his heart by the Holy Spirit of God, he ends up being divisive, splitting churches, smearing his colleagues when they happen not to see everything his way. He ends up showing unlove and God is not glorified—he is defamed.

Christians ought to love one another, as Christ loved us all. That we don't, is proof enough that we are ready to use every good gift from God except the one he most wants us to use—his love.

But suppose we do love (at least) most of our Christian brothers and sisters. What about those who do not call themselves Christian? Are we to shun them? Are we to behave when we are with them as though we have achieved a height they have not achieved? Are we to be always about the business of trying to "do them good?" Are we to have no contact at all with non-believers except with Bible in hand, witnessing to what God has done for us? Setting ourselves still higher above them in our twisted concept of what the cross really means?

Let's go back to what Jesus said here: "You shall love the Lord your God with all your heart, and with all your soul, and with all your mind (intellect). This is the great (most important, principal) and first commandment. And a second is like it, You shall love your neighbor as [you do] yourself."

He did not say that loving one's neighbor was second in importance, he said it was "a second *like* it." Of equal importance with loving God is loving our neighbor!

Now, if we think this through, we know that when Jesus was on earth, giving his commandments, everyone did not have a believing neighbor. Things were pretty much then as they are now. This is no credit to the contagion of our brand of Christianity, but it is still true that we don't all have Christian neighbors. In fact, our "neighbor," as Jesus meant it here, does not have to live next door or even down the block. *Our neighbors are all the other human beings on earth.* We are earth neighbors and, according to Jesus, we are to love our earth neighbors just the way we love ourselves: Jewish neighbors, Japanese neighbors, Negro neighbors, Italian neighbors, Swedish neighbors, Russian neighbors, Chinese neighbors, British neighbors—all of them.

And to love our neighbors means to take willing *responsibility* for them.

If we are to love with the very love of God which *has been* "shed abroad in our hearts" by the Holy Spirit (or Paul was wrong), then we are to take responsibility for them as God has taken responsibility for us.

I do not understand very much about the caliber of God's responsibility yet. I am learning. It has my attention. But I do know that he not only assumed the terrible responsibility of having created mankind in the first place, he carried that responsibility on through the Old Testament era by way of the prophets, made it unmistakably clear to the whole world when he hung on the cross in the person of his Son, Jesus Christ, and carries it on today through his Holy Spirit.

Now, God did not just assume responsibility for his *followers* or make clear the extent of his responsibility to a select few. "For God so greatly loved *and* dearly prized the world that He [even] gave up His only-begotten (unique) Son, so that whoever believes in (trusts, clings to, relies on) Him shall not perish—come to destruction, be lost—but have eternal (everlasting) life."

Do we, who have begun to trust, to cling to, to rely upon —to make *use of* his love, really show love to everyone?

There was once a hard-working, "constantly serving" woman who always made a casserole dish and took it over to welcome every new person who moved into her neighborhood. She not only did this with great regularity, she let everyone in her church, including the pastor, know of her good works. Then one day she came bustling into the parsonage, her face flushed with anger and deflated dignity: a new neighbor had moved next door and the reputation of the new neighbor as a "loose woman" brought the good services of the self-righteous sister to a screeching halt. *"Me* make a casserole for *that* woman? Why, it's going to be bad enough to have to live next door to her!"

Nothing her minister could say budged her. She was "responsible" only toward the new neighbor who pleased and agreed with *her.* No attitude of heart could be further from the attitude of God and this would be a fine time for us to stop and be grateful that this is true. Suppose God acted with responsibility only toward those of us who pleased him!

To be responsible, we must fulfill our love obligations to every person with whom we come in contact. And this means far more than "running over with a hot dish" of something, although there are times when an act of that kind can be the highest indication of responsible love. If "running over with a hot dish" is a self-righteous fetish, no. If a need is being met and our motive is the motive of love, yes.

But many who consider themselves sincere Christians keep what they call their "peace of mind" by living round and round within the circumspect circle of their own kind, completely ignoring their *responsibility* to those outside:

I don't read the papers any more, and when my husband puts the news on TV I walk right out of the room. There's just too much horrible stuff going on in our world for me!

I declare, I wish they'd stop all this marching and throwing rocks. Why, you never saw a friendship like the one I have with my colored cook. It's high time somebody stopped all this outside agitation.

I hate communism as much as anyone hates it, but after all, we don't know those Vietnamese people—and Viet Nam is so far away!

I decry all the agitation too, and there is no doubt that there is outside agitation in the Civil Rights movement in America. But does this dismiss me from my responsibility to do whatever I can do to bring about equality and justice? And if I love as God has instructed, aren't the Vietnamese people my neighbors? My neighbors whom I am to love, to be concerned for, to care about as I care about myself?

I do not believe God was propagating the kind of love that just sits at home and "broadcasts" itself. Real love reaches actively toward the loved one with concrete help, but it reaches in the spirit of the One who is always reaching toward his world.

"Little children, let us not love [merely] in theory or in speech but in deed and in truth—in practice and in sincerity."

How can we *reach* concretely? How can we *love* "in practice and in sincerity?" One way, surely, is not to gripe about the increased taxes which will go to improve the lot of our Vietnamese neighbors. We can also buy wheel chairs and adopt Vietnamese orphans and widows through World Vision and other charitable organizations. We can write letters to our servicemen who are risking their lives to insure freedom for these beautiful, war-weary Asian people. And we can pray, but God can more readily answer the prayers of those who actively *do* what they are able to do.

Responsible love is a far different thing from what most of us consider *loving* to be. *Responsible love* is not simply doling out gifts of material things or money. Material gifts can harm the objects of our love unless the very nature of the love we offer causes them to want to become their best selves. If Americans, through their government and their gifts, can inspire the Vietnamese or any of the other struggling people of the world to want to learn to be self-supporting, to want to find true freedom, then Americans will be loving responsibly as God would have us love.

When we simply give, permitting stultifying dependence, we hurt the recipients of our gifts. When we give, demanding that they begin to do things our way, we cause only bondage. Russia and Red China give to bind, and perhaps America, on the other hand, has at times been guilty of having given so freely as to cause stultifying dependence.

Responsible love always cares about the end result for the loved one.

For example, the parent who truly loves a child, does not weep and become depressed when the child is grown and away from home, no longer dependent. The parent who truly loves rejoices when that times comes, because this is what all the years' love and caring and guidance have been intended to do: to give freedom and responsible maturity to the child, to get him ready for living his *own life*. The mother who does not rejoice at seeing the child go out independent of her care, ready for life, loves herself more than she loves her child. If this sounds a bit hard, I refer you to Anna Mow's unusual book: *Your Teen-ager And You.* She is a mother and a grandmother and has earned the right to say it.

To live circumspectly, within the safe boundaries of either our homes or our churches, ignoring the call to responsibility outside is *not* to follow the command of Jesus. "My children have always had my attention. I have never stinted my children's needs." But what about the needs outside your family? "I'm one of those who never misses a Sunday. I love my church. It is my whole life. I'm serving on nine committees this year!" But what about the needs outside your church?

Responsible Christians are balanced. They neither overdo nor underdo. In fact, although we must place our willingness to act behind our love, truly responsible persons have long ago learned that before the *doing* must come the *being*.

Much has been said and written on the shocking lack of responsibility which seems to be infecting all human beings where their fellow citizens are concerned. You recall reading about the brutal murder of the Genovese girl in New York who was stabbed to death in full view of her neighbors. Recently I learned of another similar tragedy. A lady called the home of distant relatives of mine, to report the lights had been burning for several nights in their summer cottage outside the city where they live. The husband, an elderly man, drove to the cottage to investigate. Whoever had been burning the lights, shot him in the back of the head and killed him. Now, the police cannot find a single neighbor who will admit to having made that telephone call. It turned out to be a criminal case and the neighbors' "responsibility" wouldn't stretch that far. "I guess you can't blame them for not wanting to get involved," the man's heartbroken wife said. But their refusal must leave her feeling still more alone in her world of grief.

Nothing that ever happens to his loved ones can get too unpleasant or too repulsive for *God's involvement*, for his willingness to carry out *his responsibility*. He is every minute eagerly taking full responsibility for us, just as Jesus took full responsibility for our sin. And yet, God has the genius of leaving us *free*. No matter how we scorn his acts of responsibility toward us, he never burdens us with his own disappointment over our behavior. In spite of God's minute by minute watchfulness, he never uses a big stick. He binds us only with the cords of love and love frees the loved one to grow, to learn, to become his best self.

God can do this because he is free not to have to protect himself. Self-concern, self-protection make it impossible for us to cultivate a love relationship with anyone. The ability to give someone the responsible attention needed to build a free and lasting relationship cannot be realized when we are occupied with ourselves. In his book, *The Ability To Love*,

Allan Fromme wrote: "Like a weed, love can flourish any-where. Even the most barren, craggy rocks can nourish an occasional flower. But specimen shrubs or prize-winning flowers require a rich, healthy soil. Personal freedom is the healthy ground for ideal love and this is what we nowadays call emotional maturity."

Here is that word *maturity* again. To welcome responsi-bility, to learn to love richly, so the object of our love will flourish, we must *welcome maturity*. "*Personal freedom . . . is what we nowadays call emotional maturity.*"

If you are binding someone's life, or keeping it under a constant strain because your love is *not* free of *you*, of your feelings in the matter, you are *not loving responsibly*.

If you are stunting the growth of the one you love, check the quality of the soil of your love. Rich, healthy soil grows specimen plants.

For the Christian, at the root of learning how to welcome the responsibility of love, lies the necessity to recognize the *one major responsibility*—our responsibility as followers of Jesus Christ, *to have God clear in our minds first*.

If we do not have him clear, if we are still dragging the distortions of biased teaching, of opinionated minds, if we are still half afraid of God ourselves, we cannot begin to learn the true nature of our responsibility toward other human beings. This could be the reason so many sincere, nervous Christians find it impossible just to be friends, just to enjoy themselves. They follow a fearful God, a God of vengeance. They are preaching the Great Commission of the New, but living in fear of the sometimes confusingly seen God of the Old Testament.

This need not be.

Anyone can now know the basic nature of God. Anyone can know his intentions toward the world. Anyone can know the peace that inevitably follows the discovery through Jesus Christ that God *has* already taken full responsibility for us all.

Anyone can have God straight because God has come straight to us in Jesus Christ. "He has revealed Him."

Surely our first responsibility as followers of the One who cared enough to come to us in person, to make God clear, is to look at Jesus and get our concepts of the Father untangled. We cannot act in the love and the responsibility of the God of love unless we know something of how his love operates. He has not only taken full responsibility for us, for our sin, but for the clarification of himself—*to us* in Jesus Christ.

The more we learn of the true nature of God's responsibility toward us, the more easily we can welcome our own responsibility toward him and the world he loves.

FREED FROM FEAR

The list of our fears is endless; the freedom from all of them the same: *we do have God's love,* and "There is no fear in love. . . ." Jesus came to demonstrate God's love to us, to give us direct access to the heart of the Father, to set us free of our fears which in the face of such love cannot long survive.

17 / FREED FROM FEAR

FEAR OF ONE KIND or another travels with modern man and he keeps running faster to get away from it.

Can we escape *fear* by running?

No. If we could, we would have managed long ago, because fear has not just become the unwelcome companion of man in the twentieth century, it has always been with him: after Eden—fear.

We are told that modern man's fears are more debilitating, more constant. Certainly, because of the increased facility of travel and communication, causing our world to seem small, because of overpopulation and the resultant loss of privacy and quiet, man's fears are heightened and intensified. Still, it is true that man's *basic fears* have not changed; they have only increased. In the main, we do not fear *different* things, we are just more fearful of the *same* things.

Man has always feared the *unknown*. Primitive men invented gods behind every tree, to allay their fears of what unknown force lurked behind the bushes of their ignorance.

179

We have discovered much of what is behind the mystery bushes, but our fear of the unknown remains: mainly a fear of what is unknown in the inner nature of our fellow man. We have never had greater reason to mistrust our motives. In a real sense, we are still inventing gods to dull our fears: gods of wealth, of nuclear power, of personal and international prestige, of success, of influence. We still fear the unknown and still invent our own gods to allay the fears of what demons lurk in the technology-obsessed minds of our fellow human beings.

Our *personal* fears, the more explicit fears, the fears we attempt to keep hidden remain the same too. No one minds admitting publicly to the healthy, commonly shared fear of nuclear war. We all share that fear together. But we are still attempting to sublimate, to repress, to push down our particular *personal fears* as signs of weakness. They are signs of weakness, but of a weakness characteristic to us all, i.e., our personal fears are *human traits*, human down-pulls, the inevitable consequences of human frailty. We do not all share the same fears in equal measure; some of us are more afraid in one area than another, but in us all are the seeds of certain specific shared human fears.

Can we be free of fear? Surely there is no freedom at all if there is no freedom from fear. What does God have to offer here? What, specifically, does he have to offer where our personal fears are concerned?

For the sake of clarity, we must repeat that, although he wants to free every human being from fear, God cannot, until he has some control of the life, the heart and the mind of the individual. I did not say until God has complete control of the life, the heart and the mind of the individual. Losing our fears is a growth. A growth toward freedom, a corridor through which we may walk into the wider place with God up ahead as our guide. No one should expect to lose the fears of a lifetime overnight. God *does* work with our minds *as he created them*—progressively able to learn and relearn.

As I write this chapter, I am haunted by my deep caring about two persons in particular, whom I hope will read it. They are not believers in Jesus Christ. With all my heart I want them to be rid of their fears, but the rather nebulous, philosophic god they worship is not a god who can free them. There *is* freedom from fear for them, for anyone, but the only source of freedom is in the Giver of freedom: Jesus Christ, the Son of God. In the philosophies, in other religions, man is told not to fear, to trust God, to seek a blissful state of nothingness (Nirvana) where there is no fear because there is nothing. But the Christian God offers to make us free of it indeed, to cast it out in the midst of painful, joyful conscious life. Not by handing us a magic potion to drink to make us brave, but by ridding us of the fear itself.

If we have, by faith, (not by understanding at first) *by faith*, placed our entire trust in the person of Jesus Christ as God's revelation of himself, we have found out that in all of God's nature, there is only *love*. Seeking minds shift from one philosophy to another, from one religion to another in their search for truth. But if any seeking mind has turned its attention to Jesus Christ, he need not look further. He has found God. He has, in reality, been found by God, has begun to be relieved of his restlessness, because the human heart does come to rest at last in *love*. And John, the beloved disciple of Jesus, wrote as an old, old man, long after his Master had gone from his sight, but after years of life lived in the presence of the Master's Spirit: "There is no fear in love—dread does not exist; but full-grown (complete, perfect) love turns fear out of doors and expels every trace of terror! For fear brings with it the thought of punishment, and [so] he who is afraid has not reached the full maturity of love— is not yet grown into love's complete perfection."

We grow by abiding where the growing conditions are right. Man grows in the knowledge of the love that "turns fear out of doors" by living in the very atmosphere of the love of God. I see no way that this is possible outside of a *personal relationship* with Jesus Christ. It is possible to a certain extent to permit our minds to be influenced by what we know of the principles of love, to practice them up to the limits of our human ability to love, but *fear can worm its way into even the highest human love.* It is our human nature to dread what we do not know; to dread bad news, to expect the worst. Mother love, when it is real mother love, is said to be the highest form of human love. And yet, mother love can dread, can be afraid—for itself and for the loved one. *God's love is afraid of nothing for us or for itself.* "I know the thoughts that I think toward you, saith the Lord, thoughts of peace, and not of evil, to give you an expected end." God dreads nothing, fears nothing. When his Spirit comes to live within us, we have access to a love that also dreads nothing, is afraid of nothing.

Only the unrealistic apologist for Jesus Christ insists that "perfect love casts out fear" in an instant. We must *grow* in our knowledge of the quality of God-love. We cannot master it overnight. It is too different from our love. God-love is not merely higher—it is not only a difference in degree; his love is a different kind of love from human love, and no human heart *can* learn of it without the direct guidance of the Holy Spirit. The arrangements have already been made for us to have this guidance. Jesus himself made the arrangements the night before he was crucified: ". . . I will ask the Father, and He will give you another Comforter (Counselor, Helper, Intercessor, Advocate, Strengthener and Standby) that He may remain with you forever, The Spirit of Truth, Whom the world cannot receive (welcome, take to its heart), because it does not see Him, nor know *and* recognize Him. But you know *and* recognize Him, for He lives with you [constantly] and will be in you. I will not leave you orphans—comfortless, desolate, bereaved, forlorn, helpless—I will come [back] to you. Just a little while now and the world will not see Me any more, but you will see Me; because I live, you will live also. At that time—when that day comes—you will know [for yourselves] that I am in My Father, and you [are] in Me, and I [am] in you."

"That day" has come. The Holy Spirit of God, the Spirit of Truth, the promised Counselor has come, and those of us who believe, know he has come to begin ridding us of our fears and our darkness, because we are *being* freed of them daily!

I am sure my two friends whom I long to see begin to lose their fears would ask: "What about all the fearful Christians we know? If this is all true, why are Christians so full of fears too? Why do some of them panic when things go wrong?"

Their question is pertinent, logical. Is it that "fearful Christians" lack some particular access to God? Is it that they prefer their snug harbor of fears to the adventure of faith in the wider place? Perhaps. But I am also convinced that most Christians who carry about unnecessary loads of fear, recognized and unrecognized, who panic in the tight spots, have simply not stopped to *think through* to the only possible conclusion; the key God gives through the Apostle Paul: "Let this mind be in you, which was also in Christ Jesus."

God has given us the key, and yet followers of Jesus Christ go through their entire lives riddled with the same fears non-believers know. They read their Bibles, they pray, they run to human counselors for the answers and usually end up with not only their fear, but an added burden of guilt. They read in their Bibles that "perfect love casts out fear" and when they find their fear returning not ten minutes after they have read John's confident words, they begin to blame themselves either for not *having* perfect love in their own hearts, or for being somehow unable to draw on the perfect love of God.

We must think it through.

No one has ever successfully plunged headlong into king-dom-living. It is a *growth*. There is no place in the written-down Word of God where we are told that anything is going to happen in a minute. Certainly nothing in which we are

actively involved. Some theologians claim that the new birth
is instantaneous. I don't disagree with this. But the new
birth is God's part. Anything that involves us is going to
take time. John wrote: ". . . and so he who is afraid *has not
reached the full maturity of love.*"

Maturity again. And maturity—all maturity is growth, and
all growth takes time.

Now, back to the key Paul gives us: a key created and
supplied by God, but a key which we ourselves must use.

The King James Bible translates the key this way: "Let
this mind be in you, which was also in Christ Jesus." The
Amplified Bible clearly elucidates: "Let this same attitude
and purpose and [humble] mind be in you which was in
Christ Jesus. . ."

It seems to me, the important word is "attitude." If we are
ever to grasp the freedom from fear in the perfect love of
God, we must have Jesus' attitude toward the Father from
whom all perfect gifts come—particularly the gift of perfect
love which alone can turn our fears out of doors!

At the bottom of almost every fear we have ever known
is some form of confusion about God; some lack of knowledge of what we can expect from God; some twisted concept
of God's justice; some fear-provoking idea that he is a God
of vengeance, ready to punish at the least deviation from
his will. At the bottom of almost every fear is some strange,
man-distorted concept of God's will: this *must* not be God's
will for me, we think, I'm enjoying it too much—if a thing is
good for us, it can't really be pleasurable. At the bottom of
almost all fear is a misconception of the heart of the Father.
And all the time, God has wanted us to be rid of our fears
based on distortions of his true nature; wanted us to be free
so much, he sent his Son to us to make himself plain! No one
can blindly imitate Jesus' attitude toward the Father. But
anyone can have his attitude toward the Father once one
comes to know the Father as he is revealed in the Son. "No
man has ever seen God at any time; the only unique Son,
the only-begotten God, Who is in the bosom [that is, in the

intimate presence] of the Father, He has declared Him—He has revealed Him, brought Him out where He can be seen; He has interpreted Him, and He has made Him known."

Jesus knew no fear because he *knew* the Father. Our key is to grow into genuine knowledge of the Son (who came to make God known) so that we can also know the Father. Not a slavish imitation of Christ, but a learning from the Holy Spirit, so that our attitude toward God will be clear, balanced, like the attitude of Jesus. When we begin to learn something of the true nature of the love of the Father as it is shown to us in the heart of the Son, we begin to understand a little of what John meant when he wrote: "There is no fear in love—dread does not exist; but full-grown (complete, perfect) love turns fear out of doors and expels every trace of terror! For fear brings with it the thought of punishment, and [so] he who is afraid has not reached the full maturity of love. . . ." *Not our love.* He who is afraid has not reached the realization of the full maturity of *God's* love. If we know something of the true nature of the love of God, we *know* that God does not punish us in the negative sense of which we conceive punishment. God, as he is revealed in Jesus Christ, punishes only by *love.* Only by love and only in love.

That we cannot possibly understand the layer upon layer of meaning contained within God's punishment by love, in no way convinces me that he punishes in any other way. "God *is* love." So how could he punish by spiteful or negative means? When God withholds, he withholds by, in, and because of love. When God deprives, he deprives by love, in love, and because of love.

Of course, if you feel that God snatches a loved one away by death, as a punishment, this is incomprehensible to you. I believe God has cures on this earth for all of mankind's ailments. We have not discovered most of them yet, but creation is continuing. *God is not dead.* No one is dead! We are alive in a universe of Life. Physical death is not the end, it is the beginning. To die is not the end. To die is to launch a personal participation in the eternal beginning. For those who fear death—either for themselves or their loved ones (I am not now speaking of *grief*), there is simply a *lack of knowledge* of the nature of the Father. The key: "Let this same attitude . . . be in you which was in Christ Jesus . . ." does not work for those who fear death because they do not have the attitude of Christ toward the love of the Father. And once more, there is no way to have the attitude of faith and trust in the Father, until one comes to know him in the only way he made possible—through knowing his Son, the Messiah, Jesus Christ. "In Him was Life and the Life was the Light of men." Christ and Christ alone can light up the flaws in our attitudes, in our concepts of the Father. God is not dead; he is alive and he came in Christ bringing the gift of eternal *life* to all mankind.

Bethlehem was the sign from God of the great restoration: we can go back to Eden now that Jesus has come bringing *life*.

"I am (Myself) the Resurrection and the Life. Whoever believes in—adheres to, trusts in and relies on—Me, although he may die, yet shall he live. And whoever continues to live and believe . . . on Me shall never [actually] die at all."

Death is not the punishment of oblivion, as I once believed. Physical death is the full release into eternal life, and the quality of that life, whether it be filled with light or shadow, is in the hands of the One who came bringing light and life to his world.

The fear of death for ourselves or for our loved ones, can be turned out of doors to stay, *as we grow* in the knowledge of the nature of God's love.

Fear of *not being accepted* haunts us all. It is true that it does not haunt us all equally, but if we are honest, there isn't one person on the face of the earth, who now and then doesn't fear being rejected. Jesus has done more than enough to banish such a fear. First of all, he identified with it utterly during his life on earth: "He was despised and rejected of

FREED FROM CHRONIC LONELINESS

To love liberty, to want to be free of chronic loneliness is a healthy sign of spiritual growth. If you have decided on freedom, good for you, and courage to you. God will be right there in it with you. You will begin to love again and it will be good—like God. For God is love.

18 / FREED FROM CHRONIC LONELINESS

BECAUSE *LONELINESS* CAN BE such a painful experience, it seems important to begin by clarifying, as nearly as possible, the meaning of the word as it is used here.

I have always (in my own mind) made a definite distinction between the words *loneliness* and *aloneness*, but not until today did I consult the dictionary to check the definition of both words. Here is what I found:

Lonely, without company. Sequestered from company, solitary. Depressed at being alone, lonesome. Giving a feeling of loneliness, desolate.

And while the dictionary definition of *lonely* offers the word *alone* as a synonym, in turning to the definition of *alone*, I found that I had made a correct distinction. Here is the definition of *alone*, and you will see that its connotation differs from *lonely*:

Alone, apart from others; all by oneself, solitary.

Again, the synonym for *alone* is *lonely*, but—and here is the big difference: *alone* stresses the objective fact of being entirely by oneself. *Solitary* (also a synonym) stresses the feeling of lack of close companionship. *Lonely* (and mark this well) adds to *solitary* a suggestion of longing for companionship. *Lonesome* heightens still further the implication of dreariness.

And so, although alone and lonely are quite correctly used interchangeably, to be a victim of *loneliness* implies just that: one is somehow a victim. Merely to be *alone* does not necessarily mean that there is in any way desolation or dreariness. There is genuine need for all human beings to have time alone—utterly alone. The older I become, the more I realize that if we have learned to spend time creatively *alone*, we have been preparing ourselves for old age in one positive way, at least. There are far too many twentieth century persons, both men and women, who cannot bear an evening alone. It doesn't surprise me at all that so many businessmen drop dead of heart attacks brought on by tension. The poor fellows are with people all day long at the office and when they come home, there is the family; there is the little woman, who has been alone for most of the day, wanting companionship.

I have spoken with both men and women, though, who declare they are more jittery, more filled with tension when they happen to find themselves with an evening alone. This is just what I meant by the value of having learned, before one is old, to enjoy one's own company.

Aloneness has become *loneliness* to modern man. *Aloneness*, which, according to the dictionary, stresses the *objective* fact of being by oneself, has become *subjective*. People want to be entertained, talked to; they are afraid of being alone. We are not aiming, in this chapter, at a discussion of the infinite value of learning to be alone, although it is a temptation. But here is something to think about the next time you *are* alone: *we enjoy our own company according to what we have down inside us to enjoy.*

What we are considering here is that in the wider place

of freedom with God, no one needs to be *chronically lonely*. No one needs to remain desolate for lack of human companionship. Now, before you begin to think me glib, let me clarify still further. There is no quick, painless way out of the particular loneliness that inevitably follows the loss of a loved one. When the house is suddenly empty, when there is forever only one place setting at the table, morning, noon and night—a sense of desolation will come. You would not be normal if you did not know desolation. And it will not pass entirely in a month or a year or possibly ever. If you have never learned to spend time alone, your desolation will be almost unbearable. To expect not to suffer when half of your very life has been cut off, would be as foolish as to expect to be able to walk away without crutches after your leg has been amputated. Being a follower of Jesus Christ does not diminish the *desolation* that goes hand in hand with death. It can blot out the *despair*. Believers in Christ *know* their loved ones are not dead, that they have entered the second half of the journey, but communication with them is cut off, their bodies are gone from sight and we will never hear the beloved voices again. We know these things and there has to be a time of passing through the suffering of each new daily realization. The old bromide that "time heals all things" is only half false. Time does help in the painful adjustment and if we could only bring ourselves (before death comes)—as a woman brings herself to expect and accept the pain of childbirth—to expect and accept the pain of the adjustment time, we would be cooperating with God in the healing of our hearts. God *uses* time to heal us. Remember, he works with our minds according to the way he, the Creator, knows them to be. And he knows that time does change things, does heal. To accept and attempt to prepare ourselves for the desolation of the loneliness that follows death is anything but a joyful adventure. But it is an adventure with God, and time is on the side of the one who embarks on it with hope and determination to *expect* God to be in it too.

Since my father's death, I have watched my own mother pass through her adjustment to *aloneness* in full cooperation with God. Is she were going to complain to anyone about *chronic loneliness*, she would have complained to me. If she were going to be "easy" on herself and nurture self-pity, I, of all persons, would have known it, would have felt the bondage of it in my own life. Her life with Christ now is more authentic than ever before, and although my father is gone forever from her sight on this earth, she is forever in an open relationship with the heavenly Father which I am convinced nothing else could have made possible. Almost ten years have passed since he went away, and she still misses him at times, I know, just as sharply as the day he left us. But she has escaped (sometimes perhaps by a hair) the neurotic sidetrack of *chronic loneliness*.

God cannot free us from the consequences of our insistent clinging to the causes of our bondage. We all know periods of loneliness, but they pass for those who keep their guards up against neuroticism. Some of us remain lonely simply because we can't stop telling our beloved, sad stories—can't stop describing our predicaments. People grow sick of hearing about them, but the neurotic is so self-deceived, he or she doesn't catch on.

Elizabeth Yates, a year after her husband's death, wrote in her singular little book, *Up The Golden Stair*: "Look at your own two hands, look at your longing heart: they will be neither useless nor empty if you put them at the disposal of love." We remain lonely because we are just too self-centered, too unresponsive, too self-involved to *give* ourselves to other people. We remain lonely because, for any number of reasons, we have refused to mature in love.

Dr. John Thompson, Professor of Psychiatry at Albert Einstein College, said on a television interview that loneliness comes when a person has a chance to grow and evades the pain of growing. Loneliness then begins, and with it, loss of selfhood. Most of us want a quick way to selfhood and maturity and there is no quick way.

Perhaps no one intends to become ingrown, self-involved, but the twentieth century, with all its gregarious outward appearance, encourages loneliness. We are so busy, we reason, there just isn't time to give wholeheartedly of ourselves in love. We take other people lightly, tend to treat them as "things" to be used and manipulated, not persons to know and love. This kind of unconscious absorption into the faceless crowd of our society leads to loss of selfhood. We find ourselves running to the "peace and quiet" of our homes to escape the hectic impersonality of the world outside. We do escape people there, but the "peace and quiet" are deceptive: before we realize it, we have "escaped" into chronic loneliness.

Up and down the streets of our cities live businessmen, working wives, career girls, the elderly—many of them lonely, because in our competitive, over-populated society, they have insulated themselves against one another. Today's city dweller has developed a fear of becoming known, of being forced out of his routine by someone else's need. As a consequence, his life is empty, dull, haunted by uncertainty, so he hugs the vacuum, preferring not to have it exposed. The urban way of life militates toward loneliness in the midst of "many." It is impossible to share problems without sharing joys, and life is so feverish the lonely resent intrusion into those solitary hours spent before the TV set, or alone with a magazine. To be friends means to share, and there doesn't seem to be time for sharing. We do not intend to permit this, but it happens, and in no time we can begin to blame God for our loneliness, instead of moving in love toward another lonely person.

Perhaps we can avoid the pitfall of secretly blaming God for our loneliness, if we look squarely at the unmistakable fact of the aloneness of Jesus Christ when he walked the earth. I know he traveled with his disciples, but have you ever experienced the utter aloneness of being in a crowd of people with whom you had almost nothing in common? Almost no meaningful communication? I have, and it can, in no time flat, turn into neurotic, self-pitying loneliness. I am now blessed with the daily companionship of a friend with whom I have everything in common, but we have both known well the aloneness that can come when one is surrounded by many people with whom there is little of common interest. There is neither vice nor virtue involved here: just differences of personality and taste and interest. Jesus *had* to know this kind of aloneness because, except for his Father in heaven, for most of the years of his earthly life (one could really say for all the years of his earthly life) only he knew why he was here in the first place. His deep, penetrating spiritual insights were not shared to any degree by a single person on earth. And yet, I can't think of Jesus of Nazareth as being lonely, in the true sense of the word, which implies a kind of continuing desolation and dreariness. He was *alone*, utterly alone—but never lonely.

We are fortunate enough to be close friends with Mrs. Lorah Plemmons, a lady on the Island where we live, who is at least eighty-five years of age. For almost all of her long life, Lorah has worked harder than most women ever work, tending the livestock and chickens, making garden, cleaning the big house, cooking all the meals and caring for the needs of as many as forty and fifty boys in the Anson Dodge Home. After her two daughters were educated and in teaching careers, they built a little house for their mother across the road from the orphanage, but Lorah had promised her friend, Anna Dodge, that she would not leave the Home until the last boy had gone. Anna Dodge died in 1927 and the years were difficult for Lorah Plemmons, but thirty years later, when the Home closed, she sat on the porch with the last little fellow until his bus came. Then she walked across the road to her own house, where after a lifetime surrounded by growing children, she began to live utterly alone. Her daughters teach in New England and visit her on holidays but, day in and day out, this elderly lady is alone in her cheery, clean little house which stands in the woods at the almost uninhabited end of St. Simons Island.

Visiting Lorah is much more of a lift for us than for her, because her spirit never deviates one inch from joy. I have asked her repeatedly: "Lorah, don't you get lonely living here all by yourself after having had children around you for so long?" She chuckles and replies: "I miss the children—it's been almost ten years now, and I miss them every day. But you know better than to ask if I ever get lonesome. Of course I don't! Why would I? I've got my birds and all those little wild creatures out there in the woods making their little night noises."

And she has inner resources that do not come from this earth. How easily she could have decided: "After all the hard work I've done for other people's children all these years, it does look like I could have someone to make my life easier now—to look after me, to clean my house and cook my meals." No, Lorah Plemmons couldn't have decided that "easily." But how easily some of the rest of us could have dived headlong into abject self-pity.

Some people here are almost abashed when they visit her. After all, she is eighty-five and alone, and it can be quite disconcerting to picture oneself making a charitable call on a "lonely old lady" only to find one is telling her his troubles and being embarrassingly cheered!

The truly mature continue to grow, and growth is something the frightened, bereaved, helpless person left alone usually will not bother with. This is understandable if one has remained an emotional adolescent. To begin to grow is painful, even if one starts at the normal time. But if we wait until the crisis strikes, it can be too terrible to contemplate.

And yet God is in this tragic state too, eager to be himself *in* that widow, that widower. Not to be a substitute for the deceased loved one, but to be himself, to pour out his strengthening love, to surround with his understanding, to fill the heart with his courage to live again. They tried to do away with Jesus Christ—but he refused to stay dead. He couldn't stay dead, he was God, he was life itself. This same God, with God's own will to live—God's own love of life, is present to give back the will to live. Not to perform a sudden miracle; God never pampers, but he is always there to move one step at a time with us toward release from our prisons of loneliness. We tend to expect to be lifted quickly out of our grief and pain, not realizing that since God's way is the way of *growth*, he inches along with us. But he *is* with us.

In the next chapter, *Freed From a Meaningless Life*, I am going to share one letter with at least one key that worked for one lonely single woman. We will also attempt to look at the cruel kind of loneliness experienced by some who are married, but to mates who just don't communicate. I readily admit that I do not have the handy answer for finding God's freedom for every cause of loneliness we experience, nor does anyone else. Still, God remains God, and Christianity is useless if its King, Jesus Christ, did not know what he was talking about when he declared that "If the Son liberates you—makes you free men—then you are really and unquestionably free." The Christian walk is *not* to be recommended if God operates in any exclusive way, freeing some and leaving others unnoticed in their bondage.

The particular block to your freedom from loneliness may be self-pity, or it may be dullness—not natural dullness, the dullness that comes from never having exercised your mind. It may be touchiness, a tendency to dominate, inelasticity of spirit, lack of humor. It may be that you have unused humor which has simply been stifled by taking yourself too seriously through the years. Your block to freedom from chronic loneliness may be just plain, old-fashioned selfishness. Whatever it is, there is freedom in maturity and we all need more maturity, no matter how we count our years.

Remember now, we are speaking of *blocks within* us which must be knocked down before the Son can make us free enough to attract and support human companionship. And one of the first things we must all do is set our wills to being rid of the blocks, whatever they are. It is not enough to become a Gray Lady or a church visitor if, when you come back to your home at night, you still find the desolation and the despair that make you lonesome. Unless you bring home with you the same cheer and hope and faith which you attempted to share on your errands of mercy, you have a neurotic contempt for yourself.

Going out to other people, giving of oneself is the very heart of Christianity. It is the open door to the prison of chronic loneliness, and although the act of giving of oneself is the first step, the spirit of giving must be permitted to become a part of our inner life too. We must, in a sense, learn to give *to ourselves*. Learn to give ourselves uncluttered, disciplined minds, nourished by good books, constructive thoughts, and not expect those minds to steer us sanely through our days nurtured only by endless TV dramas, the headaches of our jobs and more self-preoccupation.

The act of admitting *chronic loneliness* is the first step toward freedom. And, whatever is needed to make it clear to you that there is a block in God's way, he will show you when you sit down in the quiet with him, and ask him to point out if you are touchy, hard to get along with, bossy, sarcastic, insensitive, sorry for yourself and so on. Of course, we all have to love freedom enough to take it, even from God. It does increase our responsibilities. If you prefer to be left with your chronic loneliness and your TV every night, God won't butt in. But it does seem a sinful, wasteful way to live. Indulging in irresponsibility for any reason is as good a definition for sinfulness as I know. But this too is a matter of choice. Remember what old Daniel Webster said: "God grants liberty only to those who love it."

To love liberty, to want to be free of chronic loneliness is a healthy sign of spiritual growth. If you have decided on freedom, good for you, and courage to you. God will be right there in it with you. You will begin to love again and it will be good—like God. For God is love.

If your loneliness is not yet chronic, and is not a result of some personality twist of your own—beware *now*, before the twist comes. None of us is immune to self-pity and self-protection. But God is there to enter the painful, creative adventure with you. He is there to give you, bit by bit, as you can take it, the will to *live again*.

If you are never lonely at this period in your life, do try to make some time to learn how to be *creatively alone*. It can save you from ever knowing firsthand, the indescribable pain and suffering that mark the lives of the *chronically lonesome* in our midst.

I once heard Dr. Forrest Lanier of Savannah, Georgia, say that we stay too busy to learn to look at a flower or a sunset when we are young. Then, when we are retired, faced with growing old, and with plenty of time to look at sunsets and flowers, we find we don't know how.

Chronic loneliness is much more easily prevented than cured —but "with God all things are possible," and he is ready to begin freeing *you* now.

FREED FROM A MEANINGLESS LIFE

To live in the awareness of love is to be imbued with the meaning of life. But no one lives in the awareness of love without taking each difficult step which love dictates. We can serve and serve and serve; we can do and do and do, but if we do not love, there is waste and there is *meaninglessness*.

19 / FREED FROM A MEANINGLESS LIFE

WE LIVE IN A WORLD infected at its heart by the cult of *meaninglessness.*

Modern man is far more influenced by science, psychology, sociology, philosophy than by love. Love can and does embrace the truth of all these, but to act on the declared findings of these schools of learning without active participation in love, can leave a man empty and haunted by the meaninglessness of his life. The average human being is not only confused, he is troubled and distraught to read after the contemporary philosopher who makes it his life's purpose to propagate the meaninglessness of man's existence. The sophisticated minds who expound it have seemingly retreated into unreality. Most of us still cling to the conviction, or the sometimes desperate hope that there *is* meaning and that there can be meaning for everyone.

We cling to this hope because we were created in the image of God. The brilliant sophisticates who, like Sartre, have convinced themselves that they have found "meaning" in meaninglessness, were created in the image of God. They have merely managed to overlay this image with their own misguided findings; findings gleaned over the years of their lives when they have searched in the half-places for meaning. America's truly great writer, Ernest Hemingway, a man of extreme passions, of high demands from life, deep caring and courage, searched diligently and found *nada*. Nothing. *Nada* became his religion. With all his human courage, it is not surprising that he killed himself. Hemingway searched in the half-places for life. For meaning to life.

The excellent minds who declare that there is no meaning, that meaning is relative, are driven to "make up" their own meaning. A man will always tend to concoct his own meaning to suit himself. To suit his own doctrine, his own philosophy, his own findings. This, perhaps, is a clear illustration of what theologians call original sin. Man wants to suit life, philosophy, doctrine to himself. Shallow-minded persons who click their tongues and rant about the meaningless philosophy of our times should stop to realize that ranting accomplishes nothing with these men who seek for meaning in the wrong place: outside God. Our philosophers who insist that man's existence is without meaning have arrived at this conclusion unavoidably. How could they end up any other place? God is the only polestar to which man can relate the meaning of life. Without God, meaning *is* relative. God is the only known absolute. If man, even the most sensitive and mentally astute, attempts to find reality within himself, he will end up with *meaninglessness*. This in no way minimizes man. It simply places him in the correct perspective to his Creator. God is the polestar and there is no logic in an expectation of meaning if it is sought ignoring the very center of the universe. All our measurements of the meaning of life come out wrong unless they begin at the one fixed point—God himself.

Man *can* be tuned to God and live in harmony. If man attempts to tune his life to man, he can only create discord for himself and for his fellow human beings: meaningless discord, which gives no peace to life, no melody, leaves no alternative but to try to create false meanings or to run.

Those who escape into alcoholism or gluttony or material-ism or dogmatism or any other extreme, are running. But we are not here concerned with escape. We are concerned with the fallacy of man's foolish efforts to create meaning for himself. *True meaning is encountered, not created by us.* True meaning is God with us in love: God to be *met* by man.

How, then, does even the religious man fear the meaning-lessness of his life? The answer is simple: he does not reckon on God. He does not live in participation with holy love. He may go to church on Sunday, he may even be what he considers an active churchman, but if he cannot face life's pauses—the silent places where he is faced with the true meaning of his existence or the lack of it, then he is forced to "make up" meanings or collapse. He is dodging *love.* Those who drink heavily, eat heavily, hide their emptiness in one extreme cause or another, or embrace one of the con-temporary philosophies of *nihilism,* are living lives of unlove. Meaning is God with us and God is love. Fearing *meaning-lessness* keeps our minds off love!

I try to be a good Christian, but my life seems so empty. I just have an ordinary job which I neither like nor dislike, I have some nice friends, but we don't seem to *mean* much to each other beyond having dinner together on Sunday after church. I have no husband, no close relatives here where I live. Life just goes on day after day and I'm sick of it.

We do sicken of meaninglessness. We were created in the image of God and if you have come to recognize the empti-ness of your life, this could be one step in the right direc-tion. But I am not suggesting that anyone begin a diligent search for meaning. We cannot search and find it. Meaning is *encountered* in the very presence of God and not found and not created—"made up" by man. Meaning is already there because God is there. Not only is there no necessity to create meaning for ourselves, we couldn't do it. God has a far better plan: he searches for us. *He* is the Good Shepherd. He is in motion toward you right now.

Much is being written these days (and rightly, I believe) about the inadequacy of the church. It is not our purpose to discuss this here, but if there is inadequacy, dullness, it is mainly because even the church members have begun to depend upon science, psychology, sociology, philosophy, material affluence, or more religious activity to help them *create meaning.* We all need purpose in our lives, but any man-created purpose, regardless of its charitable or lofty nature, is going to leave us empty inside when we pray, unless that purpose has been motivated by our personal participation in the very love of God himself. All of our important social reforms are of God, if they are designed to bring freedom of any kind: from poverty, from injustice, from secondhand citizenship. But the point here is that we can participate in all of these creative efforts *without* the consciousness of God in our hearts, *without* being motivated by love. We can expend the last ounce of energy in a good cause and still come home empty; we can, after the emotional stimulus is past, still feel the old sickness within.

While it is true that our act of "going out" to others helps free us of chronic loneliness, it is equally true that our "going out" has no validity if we "go out" empty of meaning in our own lives. When we merely *do* and give ourselves no chance to *be*, we sidestep love and wind up aware only of meaninglessness.

Now, it is obvious why those who do not believe in God are forced to attempt to create their own meaning for life. It is unrealistic to be surprised or shocked at any concept created or adopted by anyone who does not know God in a personal way.

But what is the answer to the *Christian* whose life seems devoid of meaning? How is it that so many people live their lives with God seemingly in the margins of their consciousness? Is it because something else has taken his place at the center? Is it because they simply find it easier to "act in love" if things are going well? If they have enough money? If they love their loved ones and the loved ones love them? Loved ones do give meaning to life. Life is nothing without love, and I am never surprised to get mail from single women in varying stages of bitterness. Single men too, for that matter.

But whatever is missing in our lives can *so get our attention* that we fail to realize that no true meaning can come until God is the polestar. Until we are free to take all our measurements, make all our evaluations from him.

Here are portions of a letter I received not long ago from a woman who knows God, but who only later in life found the particular key that unlocked her prison of chronic loneliness and meaninglessness. It should be perfectly clear that what unlocked the door for her will not necessarily be the key to liberate anyone else. It could be, but we must leave God free to work according to what he knows about each of us. Only he knows what each one of us needs to be rid of before we can really go to him in honesty. We can have a good idea of our twists, but only God knows them as they are. Only he knows which verse of Scripture will speak to our particular condition. Only he knows what we will fight and what we will accept from his love. Only he knew my correspondent:

I have just finished reading your chapter to unmarried women in your book *Woman To Woman* and I feel compelled to write. I was raised in a Christian home, but my mother was one of the unfortunate persons who found it difficult to express love. Probably because of this, and because I was naturally shy, I grew up with the same difficulty. I had a weight problem due to an underactive thyroid and a bad habit of eating when I was frustrated or trying to put off an unpleasant task. When I finally overcame this in my twenties, my shyness seemed to disappear, but I did not have many boy friends. No, that's not quite true. Most people considered me quite pretty and I have a natural wit and can be fun, but I was proud and selfish and unable to show a natural affection.

As the years passed and my sister and all of my other friends were married, I began to worry. By the time I was twenty-seven I had succeeded in discouraging all of the men I knew who could possibly have been good marriage prospects and they had all married.

I know this is not a new story, and perhaps none of what I want to say is new, but I must say I have never seen this in print in any helpful advice to single girls. But it is a fact that I have had to discover for myself—a woman who wants to get married because she sees a social stigma in being single, will never be able to call on God successfully for help. I went through this for a long time. I was embarrassed by my single state and felt a certain bitterness and anger each time some unthinking friend asked me why I wasn't married. I could not truthfully say I wanted to be single, or that I felt I was better off than all the unhappy married women.

During my years of unhappiness I was "forced" by circumstances into a great many things I would not normally have done. Most of this involved working with teenagers in one way or another, even to a summer of work with delinquent girls. Still, I could see no purpose, no meaning to life. All I wanted was a home of my own. I had a good job with a very good salary, but a career had never appealed to me. I knew within myself that I could be a good wife, and I was unable to see why God would not let me have the chance to prove it.

I was thirty-five years old before I began to analyze my real reasons for wanting to be married. I had prayed for so many years and tried to serve God, yet my life seemed to have no real meaning. I tried to talk to my pastor about it, but I did not feel he was being helpful. He quoted from James the verse that says "Ye ask and receive not because ye ask amiss." I knew that marriage was a part of God's plan, but was it his plan for me? Until I admitted my real reason for wanting to be married, I could not even read the Bible and find help.

She wrote further that when she admitted that her immediate reason for wanting to be married was her need for sexual fulfillment, she then felt free enough to find a word just for her in the Bible. God's first key for her happened to be: "Nevertheless, to avoid fornication, let every man have his own wife and every woman her own husband." This, somehow, was all she needed, according to her letter, to begin to believe God could give meaning to her life. "I had a lot to learn," she continues. "Even though I now had Scriptural basis for faith, there was not a deep enough spiritual basis in my own life to make that faith a working force. A year went by before I recognized the rebellion that was still there, and I went to God and asked that the Holy Spirit would move in and eradicate all that was unlike him."

God had used the verse from Paul's letter to the Corinthians, to free her of her unconscious guilt at recognizing her deep physical needs. But he did not stop there. He freed her of her rebellions too. She wrote to me from the living room of her own home in the presence of her new husband and his sixteen year old son:

We have been married only a few months, and have found a happiness that few couples find after many years. There was no problem with my new son accepting me as his mother, and I can see now why my work with teenagers was necessary. My main point is this: the answer for the single woman is not necessarily to try to find a meaningful life outside marriage. The fact that marriage is long in coming does not mean it is not God's will. Your book, *Woman To Woman* did not cover my problem. And I felt I wanted to pass along my experience in the hope that it would help someone else to face her own needs honestly and then trust God.

This woman's meaningless life drove her to Christ. It did not drive her into immoral activity. She found meaning *first* from God himself. In God himself. Then she was freed to love with God's own love. She did not give up and bog down in her bitterness, attempting to "make up" meaning of her own. She went to the source of meaning, man's only safe, dependable polestar, God, and asked him *in honesty* to free her. Marriage meant freedom from meaninglessness in her case. It does not always mean this, of course. Like happiness, marriage is not an end in itself. But that is not the point here. God is the point, his love is the point. In his presence, any human heart, bound by any form of meaningless existence, can find liberation.

Another woman wrote:

My husband and I have been married forty-three years. We have served the Lord together for all those years. Now that we have retired from our work as missionaries, we have seemingly lost the meaning to life. My loneliness at times is acute. We both have faith in God and yet we have nothing in common with each other now. My husband watches baseball or football or some other noisy thing on TV constantly, shutting me out. I just don't care for any of that. He has always been faithful to me in every way, but now he will go all day long without saying more than a dozen words to me. We have lost our common bond, our common ground. I try to be cheerful with him and make conversation, but most of the time I get only grunts or silence. Is there any hope that we will find meaning again in our lives on this earth?

To me, this kind of meaninglessness is the most tragic of all. When communication breaks down between two people living in the same house, a kind of singular torment results, especially when the persons involved are not young any more. The quick answer is that probably the most they ever had in common was their service to God. This, they both gave unstintingly for all the years of their married life. Why is God not taking over for them now? He is realistic, that's all. And if we are realistic as we consider this predicament, we have to conclude that there is always danger in *doing*, to the neglect of *being*. Even when the *doing* is in the name of Christian service. As long as they could discuss their service, they communicated. But they evidently were not communicating in the depths of their *beings*.

What to do? Return to the polestar—God. Not that either of these two good people has turned from God where their faith is concerned; they have simply, in the new, unfamiliar conditions of retirement, lost touch with each other. The meaning is not gone from their lives—God is still there; but it is gone from their consciousness. God has been, all these years, related first of all, to their Christian service. Now they are like lost children with no idea how to relate God to their everyday lives, minus the meetings and the demands of the mission field. A man grows restless when his active work is done, and easily turns inward, becomes selfish. A woman grows restless too, when she feels she is no longer needed to serve, but, because women are naturally more talkative than men, they don't *appear* to turn inward. Women are still cooking the meals and keeping the house, and so don't *appear* to be as selfish.

This woman could learn to like sports. It would be an active gift of God-love to her husband. Most likely the things she talks about, when she is attempting to make conversation, are not things that interest him. Neither one is to blame; both are just lost to each other. But no one needs to stay lost with Jesus Christ on the scene.

And, since the wife wrote the letter, it could be that she will have to make the first move. She apparently has come to see their need first. In whatever way she can manage, she will probably have to break the silence with some meaningful, self-denying step in God-love. If asking her husband to teach her how to watch a baseball game with him on TV is the way to his heart, then she will have to be willing to do it. My mother did this and a whole new world of sharing opened up for her and my father. Now that he is gone, she is a rabid sports fan and spends exciting hours with "her boys." If this wife who wrote the letter prefers to go on her own way, not trying to find a common bond with her husband, then she will just have to accept her loneliness or find women friends and leave him to his own devices.

One step in God's love always opens our vistas. If she began to watch sports on TV with him, most likely he will begin to be interested in her pet pursuits. Would it be a self-denying step in God-love to learn the rules of baseball or football? In this woman's case it would be. She doesn't like sports. Her husband might even resist teaching her at first, but it's certainly worth a try. She will only cause him to bolt his door more tightly by chattering at him in an effort to bring a response *to her*. God-love operates in the opposite direction: God always makes the first move *toward us*. "We love Him, because He first loved us."

Perhaps she will have to ask her husband where *she* has failed to keep the lines open between them. Perhaps she will have to ask where she has side-stepped love. But it seems to me some definite act of God-love is more convincing than any words.

Man can never cry: meaninglessness! as long as his heart

and his mind are fixed on the holy. We make the choice. Either we believe that fixing our minds on God in love *includes* taking active steps in love toward our unresponsive mates or friends, or we find ourselves having to settle for less than meaningful relationships, meaningful lives.

To live in the awareness of love is to be imbued with the meaning of life. But no one lives in the awareness of love without taking each difficult step which love dictates. We can serve and serve and serve; we can do and do and do, but if we do not love, there is waste and there is *meaninglessness*.

FREED TO RECEIVE FORGIVENESS

The forgiveness of God frees us of sin and guilt, but there is more. Though his forgiveness, in a way we need not—indeed *cannot* understand, God's love is released to us: his very being is given over to ours, so that our very beings, day by day, *can* become a response to him.

20 / FREED TO RECEIVE FORGIVENESS

THE ULTIMATE FULFILLMENT for man is to become a conscious response to God. Not to settle for responding *to* God, but to become—to *be* a response to God.

Man's very physical life is in one sense a response to his Creator; not a conscious response, but a response just the same. Even the most wicked man is a response to the work of the Creator God. Man responds to God when he prays, forming words first in his mind and then with his lips; he is responding to God when he enters into silent communion with the Father; he is responding to God in public and private worship and adoration, in obedience to the promptings of the Holy Spirit, in song and in praise. To see his majesty in a mountain, his creativity in a sunset or a crocus—this too, is response to God.

But to live one's life as a response to God is to know that one stands at all times on holy ground; that one *lives* in love, the very atmosphere of the wider place, even in the presence of one's enemies. This is the ultimate for man. This is *being a response to God.*

Since God is love, and since he did create us to love him, why do we fail so often to realize that the response of a human heart has meaning for God? We can't know what kind of meaning, but we can know, if we know Jesus Christ, that our response to the Father is of inestimable worth, of great importance to him. Most of us will agree that God longs for our response, but we dwell on it lightly, feeling somehow that it isn't humble of us to give it any emphasis.

Have you ever wondered *which response* in us pleases God the most? Gives his heart the greatest joy? Have you ever wondered how he reacts to our responses? Which one he might look for especially? Which one might mean the most to him?

It seems to me that the response which finds the widest welcome in the heart of God could be: that we would ask for and receive *forgiveness.* Not merely for purposes of our relief from the burdens of sin and guilt, but that we ask for and receive forgiveness for God's sake too.

At this point in my pilgrimage, I see us tending, in our shortsightedness, to look only at one aspect of God's forgiveness. Now that we know, through Jesus Christ, the divine willingness to forgive, do we sometimes think of forgiveness mainly as something that is going to relieve us of a burden? To make us feel better?

What about God? Have you ever thought how he might feel as he gives us this wondrous gift? Have you thought what forgiveness might mean to him? (I am not here writing about the terrible cost to God, although no one should come for his forgiveness without remembering it.) What does God expect us really to receive? Did he make his sacrifice merely to provide a way for us to get a burden off our minds? This is part of it, surely. The theologian can explain far better than I what of God's nature had to be satisfied in his provision for our forgiveness. What I want to make clear is that God has a right to expect us to be *sensitive receivers.* He has done all that is needed to set us totally free to receive forgiveness—all that the word implies. For us to rise from our knees merely feeling better must be only a part of it.

To receive freely, wholly, to the best of our knowledge of ourselves and of God, the forgiveness he grants, *is being a total response to God.*

There is far more to the forgiveness of God than ridding ourselves of sin and guilt. There is far more than emotional and mental relief. There is far more than a passage to heaven. I am only beginning to see this, but I know there is more. There is *re-creation* in forgiveness. There is a continuing activity in our behalf, *if* we open ourselves to discovery and stop settling for the wiping out of the scars of a wrong deed, important as that is to us all.

Could it be that we take forgiveness so lightly and forget it so quickly because we have not stopped to think that when he grants forgiveness, God is granting still more holy love? Is granting still more of *himself?* Is, by the very act of forgiving us, carving out new capacities within us to receive more of his love? More of himself?

Think about the two words that make up the word *forgive*: give and for. I have meditated on God's *giving for* me in his act of forgiveness. I have not learned yet how to receive his total forgiveness. Not because I have not wanted it; certainly not because he has not offered it freely; not because I haven't believed that he offered it to me. I have not received fully because I have not seen enough of what it is he offers. Perhaps we will never see fully on this earth. But to see more and still more and still more means we can receive more and still more—without limiting God by our superficiality or our ignorance.

Could it be that the forgiveness of God has been too long limited by us to the image of the weeping penitent and the benign Father?

Have we too long dwelt on the need for forgiveness for the social outcast, the hopeless alcoholic, the repentant thief on the cross next to Jesus? That the rest of us need to go to him often for forgiveness, and do not, no one will argue. But this is not a diatribe directed at Christians who grow so accustomed to their useful, convenient "sins of the spirit" that they become calloused to them. What I want to say is more positive, more filled with hope—more directed toward *freedom*. Dare we believe that God, in his offer of entire forgiveness, wants to do more than relieve our consciences? More than give us strength against the next temptation or the recurrence of the same old one? Yes. If we dare to believe God revealed himself in Jesus Christ, then we dare to believe that God does *not* give himself in small, limited portions.

I now believe with all my heart, with all my energy, with all my mind that rather than demeaning us, God, through his forgiveness wants to lift us up, to free us to be our *best* selves. Too often, we stop with the necessary first step—confession of our sin and helplessness. "Oh, God, I'm a sinner and I'm not worthy of your love, but do forgive me and give me your strength." And then we stop there, feeling lower than the grubbiest worm and as far from God. But, because we have done what the tenets of our faith said we should do—repent, we also feel relieved and obedient, and we end it there.

Do you suppose our insistence upon emphasizing our unworthiness could have been born in the twisted human ego? Do you suppose this is an inverse sense of superiority inherited from our first parents? Do we make our unworthiness more significant than God's forgiving love? What, I sometimes wonder, is the real value in declaring our unworthiness to God? Is it even a question of our worth? Isn't it God's love that matters?

If I have seen God as he was revealed in Jesus Christ, he is in no danger at all from me. Remember, God's ways aren't just higher than ours, they're *different*. His love isn't just higher than ours, it's *different*. God isn't just a higher form of man, *he is God*. God is God and we are we and only by his grace and the cross of his Son could the twain ever meet!

Only by his grace and the cross of his Son *have* the twain met. But we have met, and I believe we limit him or diminish him by not waking up to the fact that there are no limits whatever in what he has for us. No horizons to be knocked down except in our own narrow concepts.

Now what does all this really have to do with the so-called respectable among us? Those of us whose main problems lie in the troubled areas inside ourselves where we are just not *receiving* enough of what God is always offering? The simply selfish among us, the neurotic, the headstrong, the bossy, the insensitive, the prejudiced, the indecisive.

What will free us so that we can begin to *receive* God's forgiveness fully? At least to the limit of our human capacities.

Beyond dwelling on the realization that in his forgiveness lies *more* than the release from sin and guilt, we must dwell on the motion involved in his very act of forgiveness. Semantics confuse us here. When we speak of an act, we think of something that is performed and then finished. We rise from our knees after having asked for and received God's forgiveness with a kind of—"That's that. Now I will be about my business or his business"—as though it were finished. Isn't it finished? Isn't forgiveness complete when it is of God? Of course, in the sense that our sin is forgotten by God and gone from us. But the *more* is the point I would make: while the effect of his act is complete, it is also *continuing*. God remains in motion toward us. He does not finish forgiving you and then drop you, in order to turn his attention to me. Within his forgiveness, he is always *giving for* you. He is always *giving for* me. He goes on deepening our capacities and filling them to their new capacity in love.

I frankly understand very little of Dr. Thomas Altizer's *God is dead* theology, and so I have no idea how he handles the Christian concept of forgiveness. If I studied it, I doubt that I would understand. I've tried reading him and so far I have failed to comprehend much of what he is driving at. (I am not disturbed because I know *God is not dead* and can, of course, make his life much clearer, much more understandable than Dr. Altizer has made his "death.") If God were dead, forgiveness would vanish from the earth, because forgiveness is more than a point of theology, it is God's own love, his own life, widening and deepening its invasion of the human heart.

What glory might overtake our world if even some of us caught and acted upon the fact that our *God is alive* and in motion toward us every minute, every minute, every minute!

If God were dead, forgiveness would vanish from the earth. Love stretched to its ultimate dimension in God lies at the heart of forgiveness. And we are forgiven—that is, we receive and make use of this love stretched to its ultimate dimension in direct proportion to how much we expect to receive. Rather than causing me to feel like a worm—God's forgiveness causes me to forget myself entirely and swings the beam of my attention around full circle to dwell on him. To respond to him. God's forgiveness draws from my merely human heart much more than psychological relief and theological release—it draws *me* (my entire being) *in response* to his being.

That we find it possible to *be* a response to God much of the time is no mark of our own spirituality. Jesus himself said: "I, if I be lifted up . . . will draw all men unto me."

He was lifted up on his cross. Forgiveness entered the human dilemma by way of the Son of God himself. When we find ourselves *becoming a response to him* as we receive his forgiveness, we are simply reacting as he said we would. We are *drawn* to him—out of the bondage of our hurt feelings, our sense of failure, our personal pouts, our neuroticism. We deserve no plaudits for *being* a response to God. It is simply the inevitable results (by grace) of our discovery of the ever widening dimensions of his forgiveness.

People can be surprisingly cruel. We can find ourselves caught between two swinging egos (even one will do!) and where we could be bound by worry and anxiety and distress, as Christians we can be *free* if we pour upon the offenders the forgiveness we have received from God. I know this to be true. I have tried it. No matter what happens to me, I need not be trapped by *anything* but my own human tendency to neuroticism, my own tending to focus solely on what's troubling me to the exclusion of God. God is *in* our problems. He is not outside them. We go down under them only as we ignore his presence in them. We become ill over our troubles, mentally and physically, only as we dwell on the *current difficulty* to the exclusion of God. We are bound by our human vicissitudes only as we turn repeatedly to our friends for sympathy, or as we turn inward to self-pity, excluding God. We say, "Well, my trouble is so beyond me, I guess there just isn't anything left to do but trust God." What a tragedy. The *first* thing anyone should try is trust in God. And no matter how blameless we are in any troublesome situation, we find access to his help first, through welcoming his forgiveness. God's forgiveness is his wide open channel for his life. We can know that the Bible says he is love, but we only experience that love firsthand through forgiveness.

Forgiveness is somehow the access we have to the Father's heart. Words become stubborn when one attempts to communicate this liberating truth, but here is an almost perfect illustration of his healing, quieting, strengthening love coming to a troubled woman through forgiveness.

I know her. She is a dear, long-time friend of mine—a charming, sensitive, highly intelligent, educated child of God, who has known him with increasing clarity over a period of years in which her search for fulfillment has centered more and more on the person of Jesus Christ. My friend has never been content with anyone's marginal emphasis. Her inquiring mind—a rather unique combination of practicality and stardust—has not settled for the word of any particular church that theirs is the "sound" method for approaching him. She is widely read, rather startlingly correct in most of her criticisms. In fact, she has told me with as much enthusiasm when she disliked a book of mine as when she has liked one. I value her thinking always, and have found her to be right more often than wrong in her judgments. She has an almost uncanny ability to see through people, and yet, over the years, in her own charming way, has simply rejected reality when it didn't please or delight *her*. She withdrew into her artistic shell, a shell created for herself, and only came out for a handful of close friends. I was fortunate enough to be one of them. This woman was at once utterly delightful and a problem. Not the kind of problem one tries to shuck; she was too stimulating. But as her insights increased through her unrelenting efforts to come to know Jesus Christ, her inner tensions increased too. Disliking what she was coming to see in herself, her sharp critical acumen still wouldn't budge. She would not permit herself to become "like those other Christians." There was a death in her family and then danger of a serious illness for her, and during a time when one would expect her to retrogress, there began—with Jesus Christ, one of the most definite flights into *freedom* I have ever witnessed.

For use in this book, I asked her to jot down just what took place, and I share it with you as she wrote it:

1. The realization that, according to the neurological findings and high blood-sediment rating, I could have "something smouldering that hasn't yet become clinical" broke down my conception of my own indestructibility! My own indestructibility has always been my dearest possession. The greater my realization of this emotional disturbance, the more I *feared* I was losing control, the less I was able to help myself. I was heading for a nervous breakdown.

2. I turned immediately to Christ and gave this new weakened, undermined self to him. At first, there was a sense of security, but it vanished as my emotional state worsened.

3. Another *desperate* turning to Christ, and his telling me: "Lo, I am with you alway." But still, the periods of *intense* fear of losing control of myself.

4. As my condition went on, his next words: "For my strength is made perfect in weakness."

5. My *horrible* mistake of going to my clinic doctor for help; the ugliness of seeing his near contempt and his decision that I should see one of the clinic psychiatrists—which I refused to do. It was as though I knew I shouldn't go to a psychiatrist. My determination was greater than ever before now, to fight this thing alone with only God. *I had to know he alone* could help me.
   (Note: For her, this was right. For you, it might not be. Her will power is unusual. But psychiatrists are not in point here.)

6. Four days of a still more acute fear followed. Then, Monday night, August 23rd, when I was hanging up some laundry, *the realization came to me that I must ask for forgiveness.* I had asked before. After all, I was a Christian. But when I consciously asked this time (almost in no words), I experienced *all beauty.* Assurance and beauty. Assurance that I was not only forgiven, but somehow through that forgiveness, more love came, and the ugliest period of my emotional illness lifted.

7. Then came his miraculous (to me) showing of my *neuroticism.* A neuroticism in *me* that projected onto other people, distorting their motives, good and bad. He showed me that I had "made up people" instead of accepting them as they are. He showed me my unrealistic attitude toward myself; that I had always thought of myself as another person, had (in my mind) spoken of myself as "she" or by my first name, not as "I." His enlightening me to use only facts as my basis for any judgment or consideration, opened a *wide, new door to reality.*

8. Then came the decision to read the book you had recommended long ago: *The Psychology of Jesus and Mental Health* by Raymond L. Cramer. Just the book I needed to make still clearer what God was telling me himself about myself. I could feel my reasoning take hold. I could trust my entire life, even where I live and when I take vacations, to God. I was free of *having* to build my dreams for myself. I could take part in them with him. I would even let God do my dreaming and planning for me!

9. And then his wonderful words: "Perfect love casts out fear." It did. The perfect love of Jesus. My first reaction was to be kind to other people—even the dreary ones at work. I understood all at once the healing power of kindness: not only kindness received, but kindness given. His beloved presence

is every day more real, as he takes me over more and more. I know his peace, no matter where I am.

10. And the most important thing, which held me, even through the most fearfully troubled times was that I could *love Jesus.* That no matter what might happen to me, *I could go on loving him.* Even in the blackest times, I held doggedly to the fact that no matter what was up ahead for me, *at least I had this one day to love him.*

At least she had this one day to love him: to *be* a response to God. My friend now *is* a total response to God, so far as she has come to know herself, and her growing self-knowledge is a thing of wonder. We all laugh with joy as she tells us (laughing at herself the while) about the quirks some of us have known for so long, but about which we were all so helpless.

No matter how much we long to help each other, we cannot untie neuroticism, fear, guilt. We can only urge attention to Jesus Christ. My friend gave him her attention. He has had her attention (along with plenty of attention to herself, to be sure!) for many years. Jesus just won out, as he always will, when freedom is a thing we want more than anything else. She wanted to be free. Now she is. And her freedom came when she was ready to *receive God's forgiveness* fully.

The forgiveness of God frees us of sin and guilt, but there is more. Through his forgiveness, in a way we need not—indeed *cannot* understand, God's love is released to us: his very being is given over to ours, so that our very beings, day by day, *can* become a response to him.

FREED TO ASK NOTHING FOR OURSELVES

Only God knows what we really need, and the Christian who walks abandoned to him in the wider place, is *free* to ask nothing for himself and to expect everything from God.

21 / FREED TO ASK NOTHING
FOR OURSELVES

BEFORE YOU SKIP THIS CHAPTER entirely (as I was tempted to do) stop and think if you have ever heard of any instruction from the lips of Jesus Christ which was unwise, impossible, or only irritating. The concept of life in the wider place where we are *free not* to make demands for ourselves is not my idea. It is his:

"Verily, verily, I say unto you, except a corn of wheat fall into the ground and die, it abideth alone: but if it die, it bringeth forth much fruit." That is the King James translation of the words of Jesus in John 12:24. The Amplified Bible clarifies: "I assure you, most solemnly I tell you, Unless a grain of wheat falls into the earth and dies, it remains [just one grain: never becomes more but lives] by itself alone. But if it dies, it produces many others *and* yields a rich harvest."

This is perhaps the strictest message Jesus left with us. At least, it is the one most avoided by us all, most disagreed with by us all, if we are honest. Oh, we agree in principle. We say, yes, I know, I must not be selfish; I know I must give up myself, but we usually end up giving up a few *things* disapproved of by our particular religious environment and go right on—not only asking, but expecting life to give us what we *want*.

Jesus, being the Son of God, no less than the Creator himself, of course, saw life the *way it is*. He was not only there in the beginning, he is the beginning. "In the beginning (before all time) was the Word [Christ], and the Word was with God, and the Word was God Himself. He was present originally with God. All things were made and came into existence through Him; and without Him was not even one thing made that has come into being."

I like the poetry of the King James here: "All things were made by him; and without him was not anything made that was made."

Whether poetry or elucidation (as in the Amplified) it is a fact that Christ, the Word of God to us, knew every simple and complex principle behind creation itself. Knowing this, being one with the Creator God, he understood not only about the productive cycle of a grain of wheat, he also understood that the same principle carries over into human life if it is to be productive. This was no mystery to him. And of course, it was no philosophy laid down merely to confound us and make us struggle. As with every other word Jesus spoke, this too, is to *free us*. This too, is to set us free to receive—not the worst, but the best from life. The only way to realize our most productive, our most creative selves is first of all to give ourselves over to the growing conditions of God.

We tend to want to put our "selves"—our precious grains of wheat in stoppered bottles, set in rows on safe shelves, where nothing can disturb them. Jesus says we have it all wrong. And "in him was life" itself. No one understands the principles of an intricate machine like its inventor understands them. God thought us up in the first place and he, not man, knows best how we will function to the limits of our capabilities.

Enough of that. God is God and that should be sufficient to cause us to obey him. It is in some things. We can even manage to obey him in his direction to give up what we want, providing it is big enough, dramatic enough to rally our noble natures. A woman gives up her husband or her son to go to war. Is this what Jesus meant? In a way, yes. But after all, does the wife or mother really have a choice? I mean as far as the fact of the draft is concerned? The young man simply has to go to war. Mothers and fathers and wives and sweethearts and sisters choke back their tears and wave good-by and the young man is gone. Not because they have given him up, but because the Armed Forces took him. Now, this does not diminish their nobility, these parents and wives and sweethearts and sisters. But it is easy for us to confuse issues here. The mother who *gives up* her son into the keeping of God, live or die, when he marches off to war, has followed the principle laid down by Jesus in his little story about the grain of wheat. She, and she alone can decide to live as courageously as possible, trusting to God's love the son she loves. She and she alone decides whether she remains a good mother to the other children, a helpful wife to her husband while the boy is gone. Her alternative, of course, which is in direct disobedience to Christ, is to permit her anxiety, her self-pity that *her* son has gone to war, to spoil the lives around her.

I began intentionally, with a big, dramatic sacrifice. These, we somehow manage more deftly than the small ones: the things over which we *have* some control.

What about our business dealings? Are we to permit other people to "walk all over us" in our attempt to obey the teaching of Christ? Is a storekeeper or professional man not to give his past-due accounts out to a collection agency because Jesus said he was to ask nothing for himself? Is the landlady or landlord to make no effort whatever to collect back rents? Jesus did not say we are to act like Casper Milquetoasts.

He didn't act that way. But neither did he *demand* for himself. He didn't need to. He was too secure in the love of the Father. He was too secure in his own identity. He trusted God too much, even as he was being pushed and shoved through the streets of Jerusalem toward Calvary, to ask anything for himself. For us to keep an intelligent eye on our business dealings is only sanity. We all have financial responsibilities of our own. If we made no effort to collect money due us, in no time we'd be forced to irresponsibility.

To act intelligently, keeping up with one's business obligations is not necessarily asking *for* oneself. To ask for oneself alone is to ask beyond reason, to expect special favors when special favors are not warranted. Our *attitudes* when we keep tabs on our financial or personal affairs are what count. If we exert pressure and make unreasonable demands, then we are not going to keep friends or realize our own highest potential or obey Jesus Christ. Parents who make heavy demands on the time of their grown children, busy with their own lives, are directly disobedient to what Jesus said. Married couples who unload their youngsters onto the grandparents with no thought of the inconvenience to the older people, are directly disobedient to what Jesus said.

Well-meaning (whatever that implies) Christians, who begin to concentrate, even on the fruits of their own religious activities, expecting or demanding praise—soon stop producing. I dare not allow myself to believe, just because I receive a letter telling me how God has helped someone through a book I wrote five years ago, that I am necessarily still living productively. In the meantime, I can easily have refused my little grain of wheat its freeing death in the fertile ground of God's love. I can snatch it back at any time and stash it away in that stoppered bottle on the nice, dry, protected shelf. And then it can abide alone, creating nothing that has life for anyone—least of all for me.

It is in the little things, as we demand for ourselves, that we most often refuse to follow Jesus. Where we tend to ignore him. We may give generously of our money, our time, our energies, but if we are not giving *ourselves,* we stop living. And death spreads all around us.

In Him is Life.

We are alive only as we are planted in God. We are alive to create, to produce, to love, only as we are safely planted in the fertility of life himself, demanding nothing for ourselves that does not come as a result of our being in him.

Jesus said what he said about the grain of wheat producing only when it dies and releases life because he knew, as none of us will ever know, the creative principle of life. Even he had to die before we could live.

Harold H. Anderson, in *Creativity and Its Cultivation,* wrote these lines: "Growth is a *yielding, a giving up.* The fertilization of the egg by the spermatozoon represents an abandoning by each of its own particular structure and its own particular function. . . . Growth is a noncoerced abandoning. It is a giving up of oneself as he is at the moment for a new self that is in the process of emerging."

What Jesus is recommending is "a noncoerced abandoning" of ourselves to him. And I feel that the word "noncoerced" is pertinent. We may perform the outward act of abandoning a thing or an idea just to keep peace. But only death will result if coercion has been the reason. Our abandoning must be of *us,* willingly. Possibly not always joyfully, but of our own free wills. In fact, anything coerced cannot be abandoned. Abandonment implies freedom from restraint. When we abandon, we give up with the intent of never reclaiming our rights.

When we freely obey Jesus' instruction set forth in this picturesque illustration of the seed that must die in the ground before it can give fruit, we not only find our own lives emerging new and strong and balanced, we find we are enabling our friends and families to find themselves too. Where true creativity, the creativity of God is in operation, there is no end to life. *Emerging life.*

A woman told me once of the suffering she experienced every time she ate a meal with her husband. "His table manners have grown to be so atrocious, it even causes me pain when we are alone." I could sympathize with her at once. My mother kept such a close check on my brother and me where our table manners were concerned, that my brother now says he wishes she hadn't! Not that he doesn't hate noises at the table, he does: but he hates them so much he declares they have almost spoiled some friendships for him.

The woman with the slurping, wolfing husband had tried, before she talked to me, to free herself of at least her suffering, by attempting to "die to herself" on this point, believing she was obeying Jesus. In principle, she was, and her sincerity was evident. But I had dinner with her and her otherwise pleasant husband that night, and every time he slurped and shoved a half-slice of bread into his mouth, she made a point of glaring at him and wincing. I think she only increased her suffering. She was desperately attempting to follow Jesus in a way that did nothing to free her. It would seem she actually expected *not* to hear the noise *no one* could have missed.

I don't think for one minute that Christ meant for us to turn into vegetables, with no sensitivity. He is not trying to squelch us, he is trying to liberate us. It is more than death to the seed, he recommends; it is death into *life*.

The distressed lady learned the true meaning of Jesus' little story about the seed where it concerned her reactions to her husband's table manners. She began, rather unwillingly at first, to list his good points and to thank God for them every day. To forget what she was asking for herself, by concentrating on her husband. He was faithful to her, generous, good-humored, a good provider. Her list of his good traits was long. And by the time she had thanked God for each additional good point, she was rid of herself. So free of her own revulsion, so free to show her husband special kindnesses, spontaneous acts of love, that she even got free enough to speak to him about his table manners. And do you know what he said? "Well, I surely am relieved that you weren't glaring at me all those times because of something I'd

done willfully to make you mad. Gee, honey, I just don't
hear the noises I make. You'll have to work out a way to
remind me."

When she stopped hoping for a magic formula to improve
his manners, and began to allow God to free her through
thanksgiving, she began then, to cooperate with God in preparing the rich soil of love where her husband could also be
set free.

In Chapter 19, *Freed From a Meaningless Life*, we saw
the agony of soul which comes when communication breaks
down between a husband and wife. The husband was going
his way, armed with his TV and his sports pages, the wife
was going hers, armed with her chatter and her pathetic attempts to get his attention. Someone has to "fall into the
ground and die" or they will go on, under the same roof,
each one abiding alone.

> I am simply not going to church any more in her car. I love my
> church, but since a ride with her is the only way I can get there,
> I'd rather change churches than listen one more Sunday morning to
> all that gossip and negative talk. There isn't one single thing right
> in that woman's entire life, to hear her tell it. I've tried to help
> her. I've honestly tried to be her friend. I've even gone on vacations
> with her when no one else would go. Now, I've come to my senses.
> Since I can't lift her up, I refuse to let her pull me down.

End of a friendship, and the woman who cut it off is not
the one to be pitied. I think she is right. Her grumbling,
caustic friend is abiding alone because she clings to her neu-
rosis and refuses God. Oh, she's terribly "religious." She's
there, as the saying goes, every time the church door opens.
She supports a missionary, pays her dues in every church
organization, attends all special meetings, but she abides alone
because her grain of wheat is in the airtight bottle always on
display instead of hidden in the warm, life-giving, rich ground
of the love of God.

The *chronically lonely* have not agreed with Jesus' directive
for life, either. They abide alone by choice. Have you
waited so long to trust the seed of your life to the ground of

God's redemptive, creative love that you are now *afraid* to trust him with it? Are you so accustomed to seeing it on display there in that protected bottle, you'd miss it if it were planted in love? Or, do you take it out of the ground for sometimes too long a time, and then suffer the uncertainty of how things are going to come out when, in the midst of a terrible crisis, you replant it from fear and desperation? We do have only one life to entrust to God but over and over again, as long as we're on this earth, will come the temptation to fix things ourselves, to dig up the seed and protect it. Especially if there is an angle we can work.

True commitment is not a repetitive process, it is permanent. But how many anxious "committed" Christians do you know? "How can my mother worry so when she's such a committed Christian?" a young woman asked. A good question. The mother has simply dug up her seed or perhaps never really planted it in the first place.

A secretary in a Bible school wrote:

> If these people here are committed Christians, how is it that they use the same tricks as the men in the business office where I last worked? I know what they do, quoting Scripture all the while. I know the ways they manipulate people to their own ideas to get the decision they want. I know because I take their dictation!

Are Christians who maneuver, manipulate, connive, "get" for themselves (even the church offices they want to hold), trusting the seeds of their lives to the ground of God's love?

A woman said to a friend of mine: "I know my husband is right, but I don't want *him* to tell me!" My friend perceived that this woman was more intent upon protecting herself than she was on loving her husband.

Another woman wrote concerning a church activity in which she really wants to take part: "I think I'm hesitating to go ahead simply because I feel my husband is forcing me into it. This would never work because I am so stubborn." Here is an instance where a Christian is apparently more interested in staying stubborn than in serving God. The woman is obviously not free and has no idea why she isn't. There is no more anti-Christian attitude than stubbornness, which implies that "I am always right." Can you think of one which more directly opposes the teachings and examples of Christ? The liberated disciple of Jesus is *yielded* to love. The obstinate, stubborn human spirit cannot yield its life to God if it cannot yield a point to its mate. As my wise friend, Anna Mow, says: "As long as so many people stay stubborn, the rest of us had better get free!"

It is just as difficult for me to ask nothing for myself as it is for you, *until* I force myself to recall the *freedom* of the times when *I have asked nothing.* Then I have been *free* not to worry, not to stew, not to stick in my heels, not to figure angles, not to manipulate, not to resent—perhaps, best of all, not to pity *me.*

Our troubles can remain just as exasperating, the dilemma just as perplexing, but God is in charge when we are asking nothing for ourselves—when we have buried our lives in his love. Events may not resolve ultimately as we think they should, but even then we will be *freed* from resentment and the lingering depression of disappointment.

God does not ask us to be stupid. He asks us to "be as wise as serpents and as gentle as doves." The wise Christian abandons his grain of wheat to God without coercion and leaves it there, without digging it up. My life is the most precious possession I have; your life is the most precious possession you have, but Jesus Christ knows this. If he didn't, he'd leave us to our own devices. Because he wants the very best for us all, he urges us to abandon our lives to him—to let him decide.

I recently read a prayer written by an unknown Confederate soldier in which the boy said: "I asked for *things* that I might enjoy life. I received *life* that I might enjoy *all things.* I received *nothing* I asked for and got everything I *hoped* for."

Only God knows what we really need, and the Christian who walks abandoned to him in the wider place, is *free* to ask nothing for himself and to expect everything from God.

FREE FAVORS ABOUND —
IN THE WIDER PLACE

Why do we go on expecting the worst? According to Jesus Christ, there need only be the joy of expecting the best — not according to what we imagine we want, but according to what God knows to *be* the best.

22 / FREE FAVORS ABOUND —
IN THE WIDER PLACE

I FEAR THAT TOO MANY PEOPLE—quite unconsciously, have the Spider-and-the Fly attitude toward
those who do not know Christ. They invite them into their
little boxes (parlors) instead of into the wideness of God's
love and mercy. It is so sad."

This is a direct quote from one of my mother's recent
letters. Does this well-intentioned blindness among Christians
grieve you too? If it causes us sorrow, I can't imagine how
it must grieve the God whose love and mercy and grace we
keep (however inadvertently) *from* those who need him
so much.

The most grief-provoking aspect of this cogent comment is
that the very Christians who have the Spider-and-the-Fly
attitude are not only the people who have truth to offer those
in need, they are almost always the ones who "work" at it
the hardest. They are too often the sincere, tense souls who
proclaim the joy of the Lord, but who seldom demonstrate

it. They appear to be bound by the very faith which they preach as potentially able to liberate, to set free.

I have lived among the saints now for seventeen years, and because of an almost constant travel schedule, I have come to know them and to love many of them deeply. Before I say more, I want to make it perfectly clear that *all* conscientious, evangel-minded believers are *not* caught in the Spider-and-the-Fly rigidity. It is as my mother says, that "too many" *are* caught.

Why is this true?

I have thought about it, struggled with it now, for many years. It *is* true, but I cannot just let it go without attempting to think it through, because I know the hearts of some of God's people who repel when they long to attract. It has nothing to do with their intentions. They mean to glorify God—to honor and obey him. I know them as human beings and as friends. I have been a guest in their homes. I know their hearts, but I also have been exposed over and over again in their presence to the same strained lack of joy and confidence in God himself, that helped keep my heart closed against him for thirty-three years of my own life.

Doesn't the tragedy lie in the fact that many Christians seem not to experience *to any communicable degree*, the freedom of the Lord? Doesn't the tragedy lie in preaching grace and living judgment? Doesn't the tragedy lie in the very fact that these sincere followers of Jesus Christ propagate God's grace while they live in a futile (for any man) attempt to obey the Law? Jesus Christ came to fulfill the Law himself; to make it clear that obedience to the Law is necessary, but to make it equally clear that God realized man's helplessness to keep it; realized it so profoundly that he sent help to us all in the person of the Savior. Can any man really *keep* the Law of God? Well, then, how is it that so many Christians preach grace and still live by the regional, near folk-laws of their own making? No one can abide by the whole Law of God without grace, and so I suppose these sincere people figure they will set up or carry on some observable man-made *i*'s to dot and *t*'s to cross. But why, then, do they talk so much about grace? If we are still living solely in the Old Testament era where man struggled vainly with the Law of God, then buried it under a load of new laws of his own making to relieve his conscience for not having been able to keep God's Law, where does Jesus Christ come in?

Now, in no way am I diminishing the validity of the Old Testament. Without it as a foundation for our understanding of the New, we would have merely a cult of Christianity. If it were not made plain by God in the Old Testament that through the centuries he has been about the matter of bringing redemption for mankind, we would have no truth on which to stand where the identity of Christ is concerned.

But Jesus Christ, the Messiah has come!

We are blessed to be born in the era after his coming, after his life on earth, his death, his resurrection. We are blessed to be born in the era of human history when through his Holy Spirit, he has worked out a way to be in us all, to guide us, to comfort us, to teach us, to give his joy. We are *Christians*. Shouldn't this show in the freedom in which we live our daily lives? In the quiet, unstrained confidence of our faith? We are Christians who have been given not only joy, but the peace of God through his Son, Jesus Christ. We have Christ's own word for it. How, then, can we be tight-lipped and tense, socially uneasy except in the company of other like-minded Christians, going about the world as though we feared the crack of doom at any moment, as though, should God speak anew, it would be in some frightening, vengeful way? Why do we go about among those who are in darkness, looking and talking and acting as though we are afraid of *freedom*? As though we are afraid of the very gift of it Jesus offered to anyone who believed. Do you understand why it is that so many of us *cast out*, when on the cross, Jesus opened his arms to the whole world? Do you understand why so many of us *repel* when we could draw? Why so many of us condemn when Christ said he did not come to condemn but to save? Do you have any notion at all why so many of us live our interpersonal relationships and conduct our businesses on an "eye for an eye and a tooth for a tooth" basis when Jesus said we were to turn the other cheek and love our enemies? Do you have a theory concerning the fact that when some of us get an inkling of the whole truth, we so quickly turn into stone throwers when the Lord we follow was a lover? *Is* a lover?

I confess sometimes it is all a tragic mystery to me. There are times when there seems to be no answer at all, and yet, there must be one. Of course, it is simple to say that the old swinging human ego gets involved. Man catches onto a truth and it puffs him up. Well, Paul says Christians are *not* puffed up. That is, they are not puffed up if they *love*. Still, many of us are literally stubborn about the truths we have been given. Even those of us who see God's love as supreme, can become puffed up and stubborn over our *given* insight. Why is this? Human ego *is* involved. It has always been involved, or our first parents would not have been expelled from the garden and Christ would not have needed to die. But to say this is the whole answer is to over-simplify, to decide too quickly. There must be more. Merely to blame our human egos is a generality. God makes his best progress with us when we are specific.

It is quite true that if we love, if we are permitting the holy love of God himself, shed abroad in our hearts by his Spirit, to act freely through us, then we do not cast out, we are not stubborn, we do not exclude, we *cannot* repel. "I if I be lifted up . . . will *draw* . . . ," Jesus said. The love of God never repels. It always draws. So, it must be that we do not demonstrate enough of this love ourselves, if men are not being drawn to Christ.

I believe this, but I also believe there is a more profound, much more basic and fundamental reason: we have, none of us, yet learned enough of what our God is *really like*.

The Holy Spirit does not enter a man like a stream of water through a garden hose. He does not flow through us in love as water flows through a hose, using the hose merely as a channel. I've heard it expressed that way and I think I once believed this over-simplification myself. I now know that the love of God acting through us does *not* merely flow through us as channels, leaving us alone as it flows! The garden hose may not be affected one way or another by the water, but where the Holy Spirit is, there is *change*, if he is allowed to move. He will not flow through us to bless someone else unless we cooperate in the process, unless we get involved. When we take a step, it is said that the whole Trinity moves with us, but God cannot move against his own knowledge of human nature and against his own concept of love.

How can the Holy Spirit move with the tense, argumentative "Christian" who invites the non-believer into his own little citadel where his own prohibitions and pet dogmas reign supreme? God cannot and will not be limited. The only "limitation" the Bible places on a man's life in God is that he have faith in Jesus Christ as his Lord and his Savior. And this is not a limitation, it is the *only open door* available to anyone. Jesus Christ said he would build his church on the fact of his deity. When Peter said: "Thou art the Christ, the Son of the living God," Jesus said in effect, "This is it, Peter. This is the *one truth* needed." And while the deity of Jesus Christ seems to be a deterrent to some, in the long run it will always turn out to be what God knows it to be: the one open door to life.

Faith in Jesus Christ as God's Word to us must imply faith in the characteristics of Jesus Christ, and he never repelled. He always drew. Jesus was popular when he was traveling about the earth teaching. He was magnetic, well liked; people crowded after him. He was only hated by those who thought they knew more about the Lord God than Christ knew. He was neither liberal nor conservative. *He was God.* He didn't need a label. He had no need for a safe corner where a handful of those who agreed with his ideas could be tucked away out of the sunshine of free exchange and growth.

He was *free* and he had freedom on his mind for everyone of us every minute.

". . . if the Son liberates you—makes you free men—then you are really and unquestionably free."

Why, then, doesn't Jesus Christ free Christians to disagree in love, to shun prejudice, to be sensitive, to share the sheer joy of *knowing God?* Why is it then that the one common indictment against us by the rest of the world is that we tend to huddle in our little parlors in self-righteous intensity over the God who said he came to set men free to live their lives in his strength and his love and his balance?

I believe it is because Christians have accepted dogma and the call to service, and have neither taken the time nor the trouble to discover what God *is really like.*

The Bible tells us that no man has seen God at any time. It also tells us that the Son has revealed him, has made him known. Why do we go on trying to patch up our own concept of the Father from what *we* can manage to understand from man, when Jesus has already been here on our earth demonstrating, teaching, clarifying what the Father is like?

When Jesus stood up in the synagogue in his home town of Nazareth to read from the Isaiah scroll, this is what he read: "The Spirit of the Lord [is] upon Me, because He has anointed Me [the Anointed One, the Messiah] to preach the good news (the Gospel) to the poor; He has sent Me to announce release to the captives, and recovery of sight to the blind; to send forth delivered those who are oppressed—who are downtrodden, bruised, crushed and broken down by calamity. . . ." So far, we have based this book on that much of what Jesus read that day in Nazareth. We have tried to show something of *how* he sends us forth delivered from our human bondage.

But Jesus, who knew God as no man knew him, did not stop reading there from the Isaiah scroll. Before he sat down, he also read: "To proclaim the accepted and acceptable year of the Lord—*the day when salvation and the free favors of God profusely abound.*"

That day has come! That day when the *free favors of God* abound is here because Jesus, the Messiah, the Anointed One has come. He brought the free favors of God with him. And he brought them for everyone who would ever live anywhere in the world.

Christ appears in the Old Testament. Not by the name Jesus Christ, as we know him, but as God appearing to man in a time of great need, or at a time when God needed to make his purpose entirely clear. But in the era of the New Testament, the Anointed One came to live his daily life on earth and, as I see it, no one ever again need have a question about the nature or the intention of God. He (Jesus Christ) has revealed him, has made him known.

Why, then, do we stop short of joy? Of freedom? Why do we bear down on our prohibitions, our near threats of God's vengeance upon those who do not toe the mark as *we* toe it?

Did Jesus say anything about the vengeance of God? He spoke of the judgment of God, but even here he said that the Father had put all judgment into *his* (Christ's) hands. It is as though the Lord Jesus says: "Your hearts can rest, I and the Father are one. He trusts me utterly to represent him in all things." With all clarity, Jesus Christ assures us that the Father is not vengeful, is not going to "get even" with anyone. We are told in Luke's gospel that after Jesus read the sentence about the "free favors of God" from the Isaiah scroll that day in the Nazarene synagogue, ". . . He rolled up the book, and gave it back to the attendant and *sat down*." He *ended* his reading on the glad announcement that he had come "To proclaim . . . the day when salvation and the *free favors* of God (would) profusely abound." His final word was on the theme of God's *free favors* to man. Jesus stopped reading from the Isaiah scroll seemingly in the middle of a sentence! On the scroll it read like this: "To proclaim the acceptable year of the Lord—the year for His favor—*and* the day of vengeance of our God." Jesus *omitted*—"the day of vengeance of our God." Jesus, the Messiah, had come, with

God's message of love and forgiveness that could wipe vengeance forever from the mind of man!

The Son alone knew the Father. He came to *show us* the Father and so, it should be plain to us that if the Father has given the responsibility of *judging* us into the hands of the Son, then the heart, the attitudes, the intentions of the Father toward us are one and the same as the intentions of the Son— to save, not to avenge; to give abundant life, to make *free*— not to bind.

I certainly realize that many seemingly joyless Christians— the nervous, anxious, dogmatic ones, have a quite understandable fear of humanizing the Lord Jesus, of seeming to rob him of his deity, of suggesting, perhaps, the danger of excessive familiarity, a lack of awe at his Godhood, if they show too much joy and freedom. They fear diminishing the holiness of God. But through this fear, however understandable it may be, they manage to create an atmosphere of tense piety, an attitude of *unhealthy*, unscriptural fear toward the Lord who said he would "rejoice over us with singing," and who left his own joy with us. The rigid, tightly bound Christian belittles the Lord who declared that if *he* made a man free, he would be free indeed. Jesus did not offer license (freedom abused), he offered Holy Spirit-controlled liberty, where man is free to *grow*.

It seems to me that Jesus made a point of rolling up the Isaiah scroll in the middle of the sentence where it departed from the true nature of God as it is revealed in Jesus Christ. At that time the Jews had every reason to hope and to expect that the Lord God would seek vengeance on their enemies. After all, they were his chosen people, and they had lived their lives persecuted by their enemies, in bondage to enemy nations. As they saw it, the promised Messiah would "get even" for them, would avenge them. After all, they lived by the law of "an eye for an eye and a tooth for a tooth."

But when Jesus, the Messiah, came, man was given access to a clearer view of God's purpose. Certainly now, in retrospect, we can see that not only was God's plan through

Christ, *not* to seek vengeance, it did not even include *condemnation.* Jesus left no chance for confusion here: he said of himself that he came not to condemn but to save.

Everything needed is clarified now that the Messiah—promised throughout the Old Testament, has come *demonstrating* the all-inclusive love and longing of the Father's heart. To see that many of God's people still apparently do not realize this, *could* be the key to understanding the joyless lack of contagion among the sincere sometimes suspicious believers who seemingly *cannot* be free in their joy in God himself.

Jesus alone knew the Father. He had come from God. He was one with God. "Without him (Jesus Christ) was not anything made that was made." Christ was there "while as yet he (God) had not made the earth, nor the fields, nor the highest part of the dust of the world." Christ was there "when he prepared the heavens . . . when he set a compass upon the face of the depth; when he established the clouds above; when he strengthened the fountains of the deep. . . ."

Do you think Jesus did enough to clarify the Father once and for all? Do you believe there is no longer any need for confusion? I believe there is no longer any need for confusion, nor any need for us to attempt to box God into our own small, legalistic concepts of him. God is knowable in Jesus Christ—*as he really is.* Why do we go on expecting the worst? According to Jesus Christ, there need only be the joy of expecting the best—not according to what we imagine we want, but according to what God knows to *be* the best. And herein lies the *liberty*: when we are *free* to let God decide, we are *free* of every characteristic that binds and hampers our steady growth into his mature, responsible sons and daughters. Jesus came proclaiming the joy of living in the day of the *free favors* of God toward anyone who comes to him in need of freedom from the bondage of sin— the subtle sin of joylessness, as well as the gross sins of selfishness.

Men were told in the Old Testament to delight themselves in the Lord. Now we can do this with no hesitation and no confusion because the Son has come to make the Lord God known. To offer man the purest joy he can ever experience delighting himself in God as he can be learned in Jesus Christ. Now any Christian believer, no matter how rigid his conditioning, no matter how narrow his parlor in which he has (however unconsciously) confined God, can *relearn* God's true nature in Jesus Christ. Now the most prodigal among us can *know* God.

Now that Christ has come, anyone who wants freedom enough to trust him for it, *can be free.* Now that the Anointed One has come to reveal the Father as he really is, anyone can *learn* to trust him. Faith is the by-product, the quite unavoidable, inevitable by-product of discovering the true nature of God.

And if we *know* God, we are free to choose to place our very lives in his hands. If we know him, we are free to choose to walk with him, unhampered by false humility, by prejudice, by insensitivity, by stubbornness, by indecision, by greed, by immaturity. We are free to live with him in the wider place, where God's love and God's forgiveness can make our lives a singular, total response to him.